Watershed – Angola and Mozambique: A Photo-History: The Portuguese Collapse in Africa, 1974–1975 is co-published in 2014 by
Helion & Company Ltd, 26 Willow Road, Solihull, West Midlands, B91 1UE, England, tel 0121 705 3393, fax 0121 711 4075 email info@helion.co.uk ,website www.helion.co.uk, and 30° South Publishers (Pty) Ltd., 16 Ivy Road, Pinetown 3610, South Africa, email info@30degreessouth.co.za, website: www.30degreessouth.co.za
Copyright text © Wilf Nussey, 2014, copyright photographic material © The Argus P&P Co (Pty) Ltd., design & origination by Kerrin Cocks
Printed in the UK by Henry Ling Ltd, Dorchester, Dorset and in South Africa by Pinetown Printers (Pty) Ltd, Pinetown, KwaZulu-Natal
ISBN RSA 978-1-920143-98-5; ISBN UK 978-1-909982-32-1
British Library Cataloguing-in-Publication Data: a catalogue record for this book is available from the British Library
All rights reserved. No part of this publication may be reproduced, stored, manipulated in any retrieval system, or transmitted in any mechanical, electronic form or by any other means, without the prior written authority of the publishers, except for short extracts in media reviews. Any person who engages in any unauthorized activity in relation to this publication shall be liable to criminal prosecution and claims for civil and criminal damages.

This unique photographic record of one of the most seismic events in Africa's long ordeal of shedding colonialism and white rule had its genesis in a small South African news agency. It was the Argus Africa News Service, created by the Argus Group of newspapers after the Second World War, that would bring news of Africa to insular South Africans. It did so with formidable success until it was sadly and, in my view, mistakenly terminated when Independent Newspapers brought the Group in August 1995.

The coup d'état that brought down the Portuguese dictatorship and empire on 25 April 1974 dramatically accelerated the liberation process on many African fronts, most notably Angola and Mozambique; indirectly it had an enormous impact on the struggles for black majority rule in Rhodesia and South Africa.

Suddenly there was an unexpected and huge demand for news coverage on the AANS which I then headed up. We met it. Often beating the pack of foreign correspondents to it by being at the scenes of action around the clock for nearly two years, sometimes borrowing extra reporters from the many newspapers we served, often borrowing photographers. At times I had dozens on the job.

Both – scribes and lensmen – took pictures, sometimes at considerable risk, using their ingenuity to take them and ensuring – from these dark corners of confrontation – that a copy got back to South Africa.

After so many years it is not possible to be sure who took what pictures. So I list here all those I can remember who used cameras. Their dedication and professionalism put the Argus newspapers far ahead of any other media covering the long-running story. If I have left any out, forgive me and tell me – they will be in next time round.

We were there right at the start but unfortunately not at the very end. Any South Africans found in Angola at independence would have been arrested, or worse, as right at that moment South Africans forces were invading Angola from the south.

None of the work of those listed below would have been brought to light today, and so beautifully, but for the initiative, guidance and expertise of Chris and Kerrin Cocks of the publishers, 30 Degrees South.

Tom Ballantyne
Frank Black
Ruphin Coudyzer
Deon du Plessis
John Edlin
Ken Feil
Peter Jordan
Jimmy Limberis
Graham Linscott
Jim McLagan

Wilf Nussey
David Paynter
Allen Pizzey
Henry Reuter
José Ricardo
Tom Roy
Clive Smith
Roley Solomon
Chris van Gas

Wilf Nussey

CONTENTS

Part I: Introduction

A background and overview of the repercussions that the 25 April 1974 Lisbon coup wrought on Portugal's colonial empire, specifically in Africa on Mozambique and Angola.
Page 4

Part II: Mozambique

A comparatively smooth transition toward independence interrupted by a shocking and bloody revolt on the city streets. Frelimo had an opponent, one needing to be crushed.
Page 24

Part III: Angola

Luanda, 'the Paris of Africa', a city brimming with wealth and potential is torn asunder by three liberation movements. In 18 months it is reduced to rubble, squalor and bloodlust.
Page 74

Part IV: *Muçeques*

The inevitable slums that seep from the fringes of cities house the poor, the desperate and the dangerous. The MPLA found no shortage of recruits in these crowded, decaying hellholes.
Page 126

Part V: MPLA 'Trial'

The public parading of eight criminals – condemned for the myriad atrocities committed in the *muçeques* – is the MPLA's attempt at winning hearts and minds.
Page 138

To my AANS partners and friends, the best

Wilf Nussey, seen here observing the dockers' protests in Lourenço Marques from atop a gatepost across the street, was a full-time journalist for 40 years; all but four of those were spent in Africa, mostly as a foreign correspondent, first for British newspapers during the Mau Mau uprising and later as a reporter. For 13 years he was editor with the Argus Africa News Service, created by the Argus Group of Newspapers to bring Africa news to South African readers. His assignments took him to many corners of Africa and frequently into battlezones, although he dismisses the appellation 'war correspondent' as flamboyant. He specialized in southern Africa while directing reporters in several bureaux in East, West and Central Africa, being particularly close to events in Mozambique and Angola. He is now retired and writes books.

- It was the day that broke the back of the white man in Africa
- It spurred the march of black nationalism more than any other single event
- It was the watershed, the beginning of the end of white rule in southern Africa

PART I
INTRODUCTION

The date: 25 April 1974

The event: the military coup that toppled the dictatorship in Portugal and with it, the world's last colonial empire.

Portugal surrendered one small and two large tracts of Africa to black rule – plus several chunks of territory elsewhere in the world, not the least of which were East Timor and Macao.

This capitulation forced, for the first time, a face-to-face confrontation between African black liberation movements and both great white bastions in the south, Rhodesia and South Africa. It was on this day that black majority rule in both of them became only a matter of time, inevitable as sunrise and in the not too distant future. It took six years for Rhodesia to succumb and a further 14 for South Africa.

This single event would result in 16 years of mounting strife that would wreck much of southern Africa, ruin entire countries, stain it with the blood of hundreds of thousands, create widespread hunger, poverty and anger, and leave a legacy of problems that hang still like a hail cloud over the future stability of the sub-continent.

Back in the 1970s not many people in South Africa and Rhodesia realized what a crucial barrier of protection the physical border of Portugal's African colonies was between them and the hungry tide of black nationalism.

The tide began rising after the Second World War when India shook off British rule, sending ripples of nationalist fervour around the world. Africa already had several independent states among its 50 or so countries – South Africa, Liberia, Ethiopia and Egypt – and some of its Arab nations were released from their colonial bondage soon after the war: Libya in 1951 and Morocco, Tunisia and the Sudan five years later.

Ghana led the charge for black Africa in 1957 and other African states, followed in swift succession, some peacefully, some with internal violence between rival factions. The wave moved steadily south: Guinea in 1958, then a flock of 16 new nations in 1960, including the Belgian and French Congos, populous Nigeria, Somalia and the Ivory Coast.

In the years that followed familiar colonial names disappeared: Ubangui-Shari became the Central African Republic, Dahomey changed to Benin, Upper Volta to Burkina Faso, the Belgian Congo to Zaire and later back to Congo, Northern Rhodesia to Zambia, Nyasaland to Malawi. But the borders of old remained, almost exactly the same as those pencilled by the European politicians when they carved Africa up at a conference in Berlin in 1884 – with no regard for traditional, geographic or ethnic boundaries.

In the wake of independence localized conflicts flared like bushfires all over Africa as the new freedom released ambitions, frustrations, old grudges and simple greed, long suppressed by colonial rulers. Africa became synonymous with bloodshed and an unsurpassed casual waste of human life – until the Khmer Rouge and Pol Pot emerged in Cambodia. The world began to treat Africa with growing reserve, at arm's length.

The wave of independence continued to flow. In 1962 it carried Uganda into a new era which soon slid into horror that bottomed out with Idi Amin. In the same year the Belgian possession of Ruanda-Urundi became two mini-states: Rwanda and Burundi, also destined to plunge into bloody misery.

In 1963 Kenya, one of Europe's favourite African countries – a model of benign colonialism, the good life for white settlers and a happy hunting ground for the wealthy – became a republic under Jomo Kenyatta, jailed in the 1950s for his involvement with the Mau Mau uprising. Ironically, the Mau Mau had little to do with Kenya gaining its independence; contrary to the widespread belief by today's politically correct historians it was not a freedom movement. Kenyan political leaders did, indeed, try to use it to break British rule but it was born long before that as a cult rooted in mystique, ancestor worship and witchcraft. But they lost control and it swelled into a loose-knit movement of extreme savagery using bestiality and mind-shocking breaches of culture to impose its power on black people, particularly among the Kikuyu.

Before the British, under the command of General George Erskine, crushed it in 1955, the Mau Mau killed fewer than 60, whites, including security force members. However, they killed most of the 14,000 or so black people who died in the conflict. Not the right ratio for a freedom movement.

In 1964 Zambia and Malawi became independent states after Britain's abortive attempt to create a Central African Federation together with Southern Rhodesia. A year later Rhodesia unilaterally declared its own independence and the stage was set for conflict.

"Africa became synonymous with bloodshed and an unsurpassed casual waste of human life."

> "The First World did not allow itself to be unduly upset by the loss of a handful of whites, however brutally they may have died. It saw this as Africa's affair. Both Western and Eastern blocs were more interested in political and commercial profit and their criticism of African brutality and corruption was muted, except when it came to their growing censure of South African apartheid."

Up to this point the black nationalist tide had encountered little white resistance. The west and central African states had hardly any Europeans who were permanent residents or could claim nationality through birth. Whether British, French, Belgian or Spanish, most white residents were temporary, there on business or working for the colonial authorities. If things went wrong they could simply pack up and go home, which many did.

Uganda, as a protectorate, had fewer than 10,000 white residents, hardly any of whom could lay claim to citizenship. However, it also had about 85,000 Indian residents, almost all of whom were forced to leave by Idi Amin; most settled in Britain where they became a prosperous community. Similarly the Tanganyika protectorate, now part of Tanzania, had few white residents.

Kenya's white residents numbered some 35,000 at independence in 1963, of whom about 5,000 were settlers who owned large farms. They were the backbone of an economy with little other potential except tourism, then still in its infancy. Many were born in Kenya and called themselves Kenyans but had dual British citizenship. Ironically, many were descendants of Afrikaners who had trekked this far north to escape British rule in South Africa or had come later to settle.

After independence black land greed erupted in squatting, rustling, crop destruction and physical threat which soon forced all but a few determined whites to pack up and leave for other countries – Rhodesia, South Africa or, for those who foresaw history repeating itself elsewhere in Africa, Australia, Canada, America and Britain. Kenya's sophisticated agriculture rapidly declined in quantity and quality and with it the economy.

Zambia gained independence a year after Kenya under the charismatic leadership of handkerchief-waving Kenneth Kaunda, soon after he and Malawi's Dr Hastings Banda

had shattered Britain's dream of a federation populated by smiling blacks and whites in happy mutuality, a kind of moral model for recalcitrant South Africa.

Thus when Southern Rhodesia's Ian Smith declared unilateral independence the following year, 1965, its border with Zambia became the first clear line of division between black and white rule.

Kaunda, however, also drew the line at being dragged into war. He refused initially to allow the border to become an overt battlefront, correctly fearing that an armed backlash from Rhodesia would devastate both his country and his image. He began a precarious balancing act by permitting the various Rhodesian political and freedom movements to establish offices in Lusaka. They had contact with their followers across the border but he would not let them use Zambia as a springboard for guerrilla attack – not until a year later.

Although only some 800 kilometres long, the border was also a difficult one for an invasion large enough to have any hope of success. Its entire length is in the hot, humid and heavily bushed Zambezi Valley. About a third of it is Lake Kariba and upstream of that is a deep valley and river gorge reaching back to the Victoria Falls. Downstream of the dam the river could be crossed fairly easily in dry seasons, but into territory sparsely populated and far from any worthy target.

So for the next five or six years, apart from some ineffectual infiltrations, Rhodesia's UDI enjoyed an uneasy peace while black and white Africa glowered at each other across the Zambezi: stasis but not stalemate.

A few hundred kilometres to the south the South African rulers complacently watched this eyeball confrontation from behind the palisades of white government, confident the black tide could never reach them, certain they could defeat it if it tried. They had huge and sophisticated military might and troops highly trained in bush fighting. They could – as one of the world's top 20 economies at that time – wield massive economic clout in southern Africa. They had a widespread spy and information network in Africa and had infiltrated their own and the Rhodesian freedom movements.

The impact of independence on the non-African populations up to this point had been relatively insignificant. There were the savage atrocities committed against missionaries in the Belgian Congo – scene of the bloodiest backlash against colonizers – but the post-independence killing and social disruption was greatest among the indigenous populace whose deaths numbered millions by 2000.

The First World did not allow itself to be unduly upset by the loss of a handful of whites, however brutally they may have died. It saw this as Africa's affair. Both the Western and Eastern blocs were more interested in political and commercial profit and their criticism of African brutality and corruption was muted, except for their growing censure of South African apartheid.

After more than 20 years of criticism, the South African government was inured to it by the time African nationalism lapped the northern border of Rhodesia. Its rulers had gone into laager mentality. South African whites were neither settlers nor colonials with access to other nationalities. They numbered about five million in a population of roughly 25 million and could trace their local history back for up to three centuries. They had no second homes abroad and considered themselves African.

South Africa was buffered from black Africa by a seemingly impenetrable ring of large territories: in the west South West Africa (now Namibia), which it continued to rule under a League of Nations mandate despite its cancellation by the UN, to the north by Rhodesia and in the east by Portugal's overseas province of Mozambique. In addition South West Africa was itself buffered to the north by Portugal's other big African province, Angola, and between South West Africa and South Africa lay the vast, near-empty expanse of the Kalahari Desert in Bechuanaland (now Botswana).

From Natal, at Mozambique's southern extremity, extended almost 2,000 kilometres of border to Tanzania, making it an effective barrier along all South Africa's and much of Rhodesia's eastern boundaries.

Guerrilla attack seemed remote – war even more so. There was some infiltration of African National Congress and Pan Africanist Congress insurgents through Botswana and somehow Swaziland, but they posed no serious threat to the apartheid monolith. They were no match for the ruthlessly effective South African police and its other security forces who used every trick in the book to confound their enemy, including assassination and cross-border raids.

■ The Portuguese enjoyed firing practice with their Panhard armoured cars, like this one at Teixeira de Sousa on the Zairean border with Angola. They impressed the locals but were of little use in guerrilla warfare.

Angola and Mozambique also had sizeable white populations, though much smaller than South Africa's, but they were very different in character and style.

Portugal claimed to have possessed Angola since the 15th century, although the colony was not formally defined until the Scramble for Africa in the late 1800s. Some of its nearly half a million whites (of a population of some six million) could also trace their local history for generations. The country was relatively well developed by African standards and could have stood on its own feet economically were Portugal not draining its resources, especially after very high-grade oil was found off the shore of Cabinda in 1967.

A magnificent land of 1.26 million square kilometres, Angola encompassed a stunning range of terrain from desert to rainforest, tropical coast to high, cold savannah, mountain ranges and vast wetlands. It had fine ports, a couple of good railroads including one linked to the southern African network which spread right across and down the sub-continent, excellent agricultural and mining potential, a small but growing industrial structure, a good and expanding education system, reasonable health and other basic social services, and a distinct national pride among its whites and *mestiços* – people of mixed blood – most of whom had adopted the Portuguese lifestyle. It was an embryonic country said to have a great future, but sadly, that was not to be.

Mozambique was much less advanced, a long ragged slab of largely pristine African wilderness with minuscule development confined to its coastline. Its economy and the livelihood of its quarter million whites depended hugely on the ports of Lourenço Marques (now Maputo), Beira and Nacala linked by railways direct to South Africa, Rhodesia and Malawi respectively. Its road network was sparse and rough, until the 1970s there wasn't even a coastal road linking Maputo and Beira.

At a few places inland, like a barrage on the Limpopo River and along the railroads there was minor agricultural development. Small ports like Quelimane and Porto Amelia (now Pemba) dotted along the coast survived on local trading and fishing. In an inexplicable twist of luck cashew trees, introduced from tropical America, flourished along much of the littoral and yielded the world's largest supply of cashew nuts.

Here too, whites could claim descent from settlers who arrived generations earlier and as in Angola they mingled freely with the locals creating a sizeable mixed-race population.

The Portuguese often boasted that their own nation was the product of many centuries of cross-breeding with other races in Portugal and around the world. They liked to describe themselves as racially free within a political dictatorship.

This was partially true in insular Angola which was closely linked to, and more influenced by, Europe than by the rest of Africa. In spite of an almost continuous succession of conflicts between Portuguese and various Angolan peoples for more than four centuries, and Portugal's long, grim record of slavery, forced labour and political oppression, by 1960 white–black relationships had been contained in an uneasy, superficial calm imposed by the iron hand of dictator António de Oliveira Salazar, Portugal's prime minister.

In Mozambique race relations were not so easy, probably aggravated by the spill-over of condescending British-style paternalism from Rhodesia and and of formalized, degrading apartheid from South Africa.

The similarity between the whites of Angola and Mozambique, and those of other colonies like Kenya, Zambia and the Belgian Congo, was that both had claim to second nationalities. The difference was that most of those in Angola and Mozambique had been there so long they did not want to leave – this was their home. They were prepared to fight, like the South Africans and Rhodesians.

Their chance came in 1961. They seized it savagely.

■ Two countries, one story. Top: the grim view of Luanda, unseen and for the most part ignored. *Muçeques,* or black slum townships, virtually surrounded the city on the landward side, home to an estimated half a million people. Above: a woman strolls barefoot past the increasingly commonplace graffiti; this is in Mozambique's capital Lourenço Marques. It reads *Frelimo Unico Guia*. Loosely translated this means, Frelimo One Leader/ship. Left: a Portuguese soldier holds up a somewhat hopeful flier pronouncing, People Unite Against Violence.

■ Left: Dr Agostinho Neto, leader of the *Movimento Popular de Libertaçao de Angola* (MPLA) and the first president of independent Angola.
■ Above: Dr Jonas Savimbi, the charismatic leader of UNITA or *União Nacional para a Independência Total de Angola*, who died in February 2002, apparently in a fight with MPLA forces.

As in the rest of Africa, nationalism had been quietly simmering in Angola after the Second World War, nurtured by a rising sense of identity among *mestiço* intellectuals and other ethnic groups, by Portuguese communists and by unemployment.

It led to the birth of the *Movimento Popular de Libertaçao de Angola* (MPLA), which today rules Angola. Then predominantly a *mestiço* movement, today it is chiefly black.

From the outset the MPLA felt the scrutiny of and often brutal suppression by Salazar's sinister security police, the *Polícia Internacional e de Defesa do Estado* (PIDE). In 1959 troops shot and killed 30 and wounded more than 200 of a crowd demonstrating against the arrest of MPLA leader Dr Agostinho Neto.

In February 1961, a number of foreign journalists happened to be in Luanda because Captain Henrique Galvao, the Portuguese opposition leader who had hijacked the ocean liner *Santa Maria*, was expected to make for Angola from Brazil.

So the journalists were, fortuitously, in Luanda on 4 February when a few hundred MPLA militants attacked a police station and a prison to free prisoners. They killed about seven Portuguese policemen at a cost of 40 of their own men.

The police and Portuguese vigilantes reacted with a savagery that shocked the world, battering the MPLA and shattering the veneer of interracial tolerance in Angola.

Six days later MPLA supporters again attacked a prison and were thoroughly beaten off. Whites with rifles, shotguns and handguns hunted down blacks and *mestiços* in Luanda – in the streets, in buildings, wherever they could find them. Men, perched on the edge of the bluff overlooking the bay and harbour, picked off blacks below like shooting sheep in a corral.

One journalist there was the renowned Don Wise of London's *Daily Express*. He was sitting at one of the many pleasant sidewalk cafés along Luanda's *Marginal* when he heard two shots, the body of a black man fell from the roof of a multi-storey building and crashed down next to him.

"The first casualty of Angola's bloody war nearly fell into my beer today," the imperturbable Wise reported. He was wrong: it was not the first. And many years later it is not yet the last.

Another political movement was the *União das Populações de Angola* (UPA), forerunner of the *Frente Nacional de Libertação de Angola* (FNLA). Led by Holden Roberto, its strength came mainly from the Bakongo people who for centuries had either fought against or maintained uneasy alliances with the Portuguese.

Once a large and powerful kingdom, the Bakongo had been split by the arbitrary border between the Belgian Congo and northern Angola. Latterly they had become the chief source of cheap labour on large coffee estates cleared from the tropical forest by European settlers – most were Portuguese but many of them Germans with questionable wartime backgrounds.

On 15 March 1961 – just over a month after the MPLA débâcle in Luanda and probably precipitated by it – the UPA launched an uprising through most of northern Angola. They butchered settlers and loyal blacks alike as bloodily as the Mau Mau had, mostly with knives and pangas because they had few modern weapons.

But they were an undisciplined, rampant mob with little training and inexperienced leaders and after the initial shockwave of their onslaught, settlers and Portuguese troops retaliated with equal ferocity, matching atrocity for atrocity. The little town of Carmona became an armed camp while on their plantations settlers took refuge behind high security fences, armed themselves to the teeth and shot anything that moved after dark.

Over the next three months some 750 Portuguese and 20,000 blacks were killed. Close on 200,000 blacks fled into Belgian territory.

That was the beginning of the beginning of the end. The lasting guerrilla war in Angola between colonizers and colonized had begun. It would continue for another

13 years, only to be followed by civil war for a further 27 years.

The MPLA expanded its subversion and sabotage largely in and around urban areas, where it had more support. The FNLA attacked into the north, northeast and east from the former Belgian Congo, now writhing in its own post-independence agonies.

Five years later a third movement arrived on the scene in Central Angola, the *União Nacional para a Independência Total de Angola* (UNITA), led by Dr Jonas Savimbi – later to become South Africa's top ally in black Africa.

As time passed, the warring became strangely balanced. Portugal pumped in hundreds of thousands of conscripted troops whose commanders rapidly developed considerable skill in the elusive business of guerrilla war. Simultaneously the guerrilla leaders developed their training and acquired equipment supplied by Eastern Bloc benefactors.

Within a few years the nationalists were awash with

■ Left: A tailless city pigeon under fire – a common leisure activity in Luanda at the time.

■ Centre: While their menfolk fell city pigeons with shotguns, wives gossip over coffee and cakes on the patio of the exclusive gun club.

weapons for shadowy war, notably landmines and other explosives, rocket-grenade launchers and huge numbers of that most superior of all assault rifles for close fighting, the AK-47 or Kalashnikov.

By 1970, the war in Angola was slowly grinding to an unusual standstill. There was desultory fighting in the distant southeast, a sparsely populated region of swamp and forest which almost vanished under the annual floods feeding the Zambezi River complex. Coffee farming was back to its normal wealthy production in the north. From Zambia and the old Belgian Congo guerrillas made sporadic hit-and-run raids into the east. The FNLA occasionally feinted into the north without much enthusiasm or impact. Rebels wanting independence for the Cabinda enclave made rather feeble strikes through the dense Maiombe rainforest from the former French Congo. In the middle of the country, blanketed by vast expanses of swampy grassland where an entire army could vanish, UNITA fighters blew up bridges here and there and shot at passing freight trains on the Benguela railway.

When they sometimes crossed paths on their forays, the guerrillas of the various movements invariably fought each other. UNITA practised this most often and appeared to adopt a mild approach in pressing its fight against the colonizers, thus causing suspicion that it was secretly working hand-in-glove with the Portuguese, a Trojan zebra.

The conflict was neither deadlocked nor stalemated but had reached a point of balance convenient to both sides. Behind Portugal's thinning veil of strength Angola made impressive economic progress. The coffee plantations rose to profitable splendour as the world's biggest producers after Brazil. More and more oil was discovered. Farming and ranching expanded on the central plateau. Fishing boomed. New mines were opened. The diamond diggings in the Lunda district yielded enormous revenue.

Trade grew. Businesses continued to invest in small but growing numbers. The ports of Luanda, Lobito and Benguela thrived. The Cuca brewery at Nova Lisboa in the centre of Angola grew to one of Africa's largest – and produced the best beer, according to its customers. Quixotically, the Angolan domestic airline ran weekly flights to Point Noire, seaport of the Congo People's Republic, and Brazzaville, its capital, despite the fact that the Congo provided shelter and succour to the FNLA and the Cabinda rebels.

Life, in short, was good albeit at the expense of the occasional bloodshed. In Luanda and the other centres, even Carmona, it was difficult to believe there was a war going on, let alone on several fronts.

In Mozambique in the early 1970s there was some economic progress but the colonial euphoria, the complacency, had been rudely punctured. Mozambique, more than Angola, was the crunch point for the Portuguese.

In contrast to their extensive activities in Angola, the Portuguese had, for centuries, been reluctant to venture into the Mozambican interior, except for attempts from Sofala to reach the remote, mysterious land of Monomotapa (now Zimbabwe), thought by some to be the fabled Christian kingdom of Prester John.

Having brought the East African coast up to Malindi (north of Mombasa) into submission between 1502 and 1509, they concentrated on controlling the coastal trade in gold, ivory and slaves in return for textiles and trinkets, and the trade across the Indian Ocean to the riches of India and the Far East.

Early in its domination Lisbon granted three land concessions in Mozambique called *prazos* in the Manica/Sofala, Zambezia and Niassa regions. These were supposed to be no more than a few square kilometres in extent for farming and settlement but the breach was only recognized when these had grown into huge properties of more than 150,000 square kilometres each whose owners raised taxes and their own armies.

For two centuries these were the only form of authority, if it could be called that, in the Mozambique interior. Economically they proved worthless: they were little more than feudal fiefdoms which did lasting damage to the territory and human relations.

The interior remained primitive, much of it virtually unchanged since the arrival of the Portuguese or of the Arab slavers centuries before them. By 1960, there were still native Mozambicans in remoter parts who had never seen a white man. Even today some of Africa's wildest, least touched territory is in the Mozambique hinterland. It was the last true outpost of old-style colonialism – raw Africa being milked by colonizers who put little back.

Not until the late 1800s and early 1900s did Lisbon begin to assert its authority inland and send troops to quell the *prazeros*, pacify the blacks and seize the land of both.

Fighting between colonizers and colonized sputtered almost continuously after that as tribe after tribe resisted Portuguese rule.

Black nationalism began to emerge in the 1920s among as handful of black and *mestiço* intellectuals and worker organizations. Their small but rising voice touched sensitive nerves in Lisbon and was ruthlessly silenced by the dictator Salazar.

After the Second World War, the tide of nationalism lapped here too, generating strikes between 1947 and 1963 by dockers and farmworkers which Portuguese police and

troops crushed, sometimes with considerable loss of life. The army is said to have killed nearly 600 of the Maconde people – a traditionally insular and aggressive tribe in the far north – when they tried to form a political movement in 1960.

A string of small unions, associations and parties emerged among Mozambican exiles, mainly in Tanzania. Eventually, in 1962, several united to form the *Frente de Libertaçao de Moçambique*, or Frelimo. Its leader, the intellectual, academic and poet, Dr Eduardo Chivambo Mondlane. He studied at South Africa's University of the

It was the last thing anyone anticipated. AK-47 bullets sang and smacked through the main building for what seemed like an age as tourists and camp staff alike fell flat; it probably lasted less than a minute. A few people were wounded but no one was killed. It almost gave the impression that Frelimo was having fun, simultaneously toying with the holidaymakers and asserting pressure on one of the country's few economic assets.

The reaction of the Portuguese forces was a hastily-cobbled plan to fend off further attack while trying not to alarm tourists or give the impression that they were losing control. Suddenly Gorongosa, one of Africa's loveliest parks, was packed with open-canopied minibuses filled with 'visitors' – fit young men in casual clothes with short haircuts. All were troops and their weapons lay on the minibus floors.

A few months later, in December, Frelimo let loose its latest drive with a shocking abruptness that caught even the war-wise Portuguese by surprise; they killed and sabotaged unremittingly along the railway and highway between Beira and Rhodesia.

Within weeks much of the gain of Operation Gordian Knot had been unravelled. Suddenly Frelimo appeared hundreds of miles south of where they were supposed to be confined. They seemed able to move freely through Malawi and the Tete district and now threatened the vulnerable south adjacent to South Africa.

The shock to the collective ego of the Portuguese in Mozambique was huge. Overnight complacency gave way to deep and widespread anxiety, even hysteria. The ripples spread swiftly to Portugal despite Lisbon's tight censorship and bland assurances.

Samora Machel believed the war could be won in the Beira and Vila Pery (Chimoio) districts along the route between Beira port and Rhodesia because this was one of the few developed regions in Mozambique and by far the major one between the huge, sparsely developed north and the capital Lourenço Marques in the distant south. Between the Beira–Rhodesia corridor and Lourenço Marques was a vast undeveloped region.

In this his thinking was right because if Frelimo could conquer and hold, or make untenable, the Beira–Rhodesia corridor the way south would be wide open. The Portuguese forces would be stretched beyond their abilities. Panic would spread.

Colaterally, his approach was also suitable for the wars in Angola and Guinea-Bissau and for the freedom of Macau and Timor and the rest of Portugal's empire, for such a setback would be a devastating blow to Portugal's already crumbling morale and assist their cause.

Whether or not his reasons about the Beira–Rhodesia

He infiltrated subversion agents far south of Tete to spread Frelimo's gospel among the locals. For months in advance his guerrillas humped tons of guns, ammunition and explosives on their backs through harsh, hot wilderness for over 1,000 kilometres to cache them in the bush.

In December 1972 a new element entered the scene. The Zimbabwe African National Union (ZANU) launched its guerrilla campaign on Rhodesia, attacking in the east and northeast. Frelimo and ZANU worked hand in hand, back and forth across the Rhodesia–Mozambique border, joining their two wars into one and stepping up the pressure.

In July that year Frelimo scored a major moral and propaganda victory. Guerrillas made their way down the tail end of the swampy Rift Valley and after several ambushes of civilian and army vehicles on local roads, they attacked the Hitengo tourist camp in the Gorongosa game reserve.

They struck in the evening as visitors, among them foreigners, were drinking and supping in the comfortable, open-sided lounge and dining room.

corridor were right we will never know because he was killed years later in a controversial air crash in South Africa and because the Lisbon coup overrode everything and virtually handed Mozambique to him on a platter. However, if he believed he could win militarily, he was quite mistaken, but psychologically, he was certainly on the right track.

In early April 1974 I was able to write in several South African newspapers that the Portuguese forces in Mozambique were showing distinct symptoms of despondency, alarm and a severe erosion of morale.

For years its African wars had been draining Portugal's economy, faster than costs could be recouped from its so-called provinces. By the 1970s, the wars in their colonies were swallowing about 40 per cent of their national budget.

Additionally, and in particular in the past year, the drain on its youth had become intolerable. Resentment was rising among the Portuguese back home as they watched their sons, barely out of school, being conscripted, shoved into ill-fitting camouflage kit, hastily trained and shunted off to defend remote corners of Africa few of them had ever heard of and cared nothing for. These youngsters were cannon fodder, a desperate attempt to beef up Portuguese strength in the field and an embarrassment to the combat-experienced forces already there and their commanders, often more of a burden than relief.

I once saw a Boeing 737 offload conscripts arriving at Porto Amelia (Pemba) in the far north in dark, mottled-green camouflage uniforms, still so new and unwashed they were stiff. The boys, for that's what they were, had been flown up from Lourenço Marques or Beira, where they had arrived direct from Lisbon and did not know which end of the world was where. They were transferred straight into a battered Nord Atlas transport, so heavily loaded many had to sit atop their luggage, and were flown into the hot, humid, armed bush camp of Mueda, whose airstrip had been mortared only the night before. The change from the placid cities and villages of Portugal must have been mind-numbing.

However stringent Portugal's censorship, nothing could hide from public view the succession of these young men returning home minus limbs, heavily bandaged or in boxes. The grim message was going out loud and clear among the rest of the armed forces too – the nation cannot take much more of this.

At Mueda, when I followed de Arriaga during Gordian Knot three years earlier, I encountered three commandos who had just returned from a patrol into the hostile surrounding forest – a burly major and two

■ Resentment was rising among the Portuguese back home as they watched their sons, barely out of school, being conscripted, shoved into ill-fitting camouflage kit, hastily trained and shunted off to defend remote corners of Africa that few of them had ever heard of and cared nothing for.

young lieutenants, all extremely fit, tough and smart. All the base's other officers were fawning round the general as he sat in the lounge after supper watching a taped movie.

Not these three. They ignored the others and took me with them into the small bar of the officers' mess. There they sat knocking back good Portuguese brandy, neat, chased with beer because the water at Mueda was not fit to drink or even wash in.

"What was the occasion?" I asked them.

"We're drinking to one of our friends," they said.

"Oh? Where's he?" I asked, naively.

"In a plastic bag," the major said, "we brought him back in a little plastic bag, what's left of him. He stepped on a landmine with an unexploded aerial bomb buried under it."

The three commandos looked with contempt at the flock of officers next door, beyond the curtain made of bottle-tops and the lamps made of recoilless cannon shell cases. "Those bastards don't know how to fight," they said. "They are wasting lives."

Three years later the waste of lives and broken young bodies for no reason other than the maintenance of a crumbling, anachronistic and expensive empire became an intolerable burden for the people of Portugal. An underground movement began among young officers in Mozambique and spread rapidly to Portugal's other theatres of war.

On 25 April 1974, exactly eleven days after I reported the plunge in Portuguese morale, the armed forces launched a successful coup in Portugal toppling the creaking dictatorship of Marcello Caetano.

One of the men leading the coup in Lisbon was the commando major from Mueda, Jaime Neves.

Peace crashed down on the people of Mozambique; overnight the wars in Portuguese Africa ended. They would soon be followed by civil wars between the various freedom movements, jockeying for power.

At Tete I wandered from the decaying town into bush where a few days earlier I would probably have been shot and interviewed and photographed a Frelimo group leader who would have fired the shots. Guerrillas came out of the wilderness to buy supplies at local stores and share cigarettes with Portuguese troops.

And so crumbled of one of the white man's last great bastions in Africa.

■ President Machel inspects a guard of honour of his men in their combat fatigues at the start of the independence celebrations, an unusual experience for guerrillas accustomed to life in the bush.

PART II
MOZAMBIQUE

■ A militiaman eyes the passing bush, so thick he would never see an ambush.

By late 1973 and into early 1974, an atmosphere of gloom was spreading wide in Mozambique. Gone was the vigour and discipline among the Portuguese forces generated by their firm counter-attack against Frelimo infiltration in the distant north. General Kaulza de Arriaga, who had led them then, had long returned to Portugal. To their dismay Frelimo had suddenly appeared far south of them, striking along the road and railway corridor between the port of Beira and its prime customer, landlocked Rhodesia.

■ It was the simplest of tricks to derail a train by weakening the track and letting the locomotive's weight do the rest.

The army still dominated most of the north but the gains of de Arriaga's Operation Gordian Knot had been largely nullified by Frelimo's ability to infiltrate the south. For the first time they were close to a prime economic region of Mozambique.

The bush-wise guerrillas were making hit-and-run strikes on farms, roads, villages and the railway almost at will. It was impossible to know where they might strike next, or to defend the entire corridor.

The Portuguese forces' response was ad hoc, more reactive than proactive, as if they had lost the will or leadership, or both. They shunted troops around without any apparent plan. If there was one it was the best-kept secret in the country.

To study the scene I took the Rhodesian train as far as the pretty little town of Vila Pery, the centre for a busy agricultural region, including thriving citrus farms and now also a military base for the defence of part of the corridor.

The only protection for the train and its fatalist passengers was small groups of soldiers guarding bridges against sabotage and a few militia in the coaches, simple men who flaunted their FN rifles with a conceit endowed by the power of the gun. What they were supposed to do in the event of attack was anyone's guess. Fortunately they were not put to the test.

There were few passengers, some Africans from up the line returning home after selling their produce in Beira, a couple of B-girls going to perform at a Vila Pery nightclub

favoured by the Portuguese troops, and me.

The physical damage Frelimo was able to inflict along the corridor was relatively minor. The damage they did to Portuguese morale in Mozambique was huge, especially after their brief strafing of the tourist camp in the Gorongosa game reserve in mid-1973. This was too close to home.

Suddenly the people of Beira and all the towns and villages along the corridor were hearing of and sometimes actually seeing guerrilla action right next door. Portuguese censors kept most of the bad news out of their newspapers and radio news but when things were happening so near there was no way of silencing that most effective of all media, word of mouth. Lourenço Marques was over 700 kilometres south of Beira but the two cities were in close and constant communication so the news travelled swiftly, inflating on the way, bloated by rumour and speculation.

It is one thing for civilians to hear of people fighting and being killed in a wilderness so far away that it might as well be in another country. It is quite another to hear of ambush and sabotage on a highway just outside your home town, and of people you know being shot, and perhaps to actually see the damage and hear the shots. It was the root of depression and in the first quarter of 1974 it was becoming common in Mozambique.

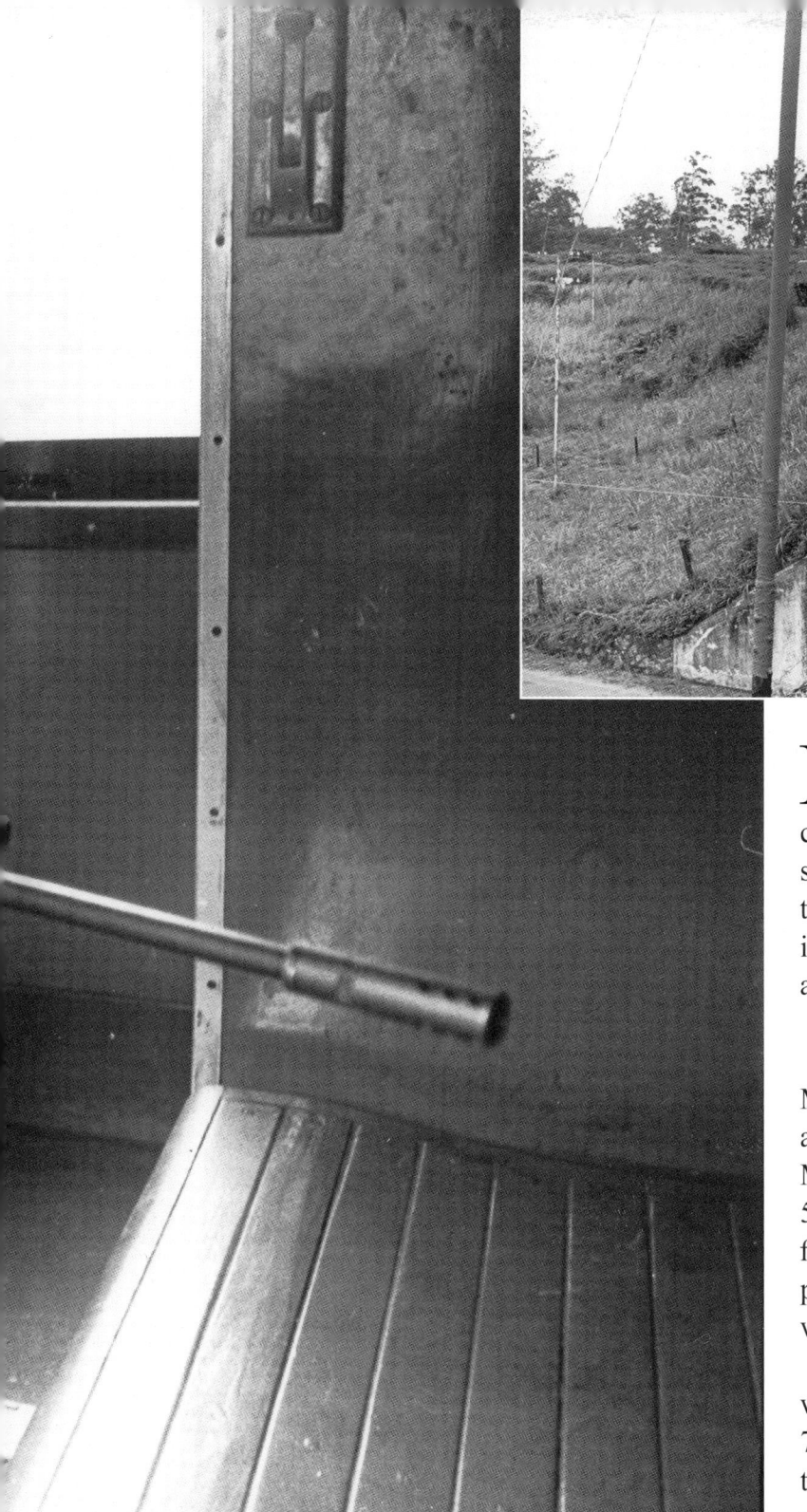

■ Top right: Portuguese soldiers watch the train pass the culvert they have been sent to guard.

■ Above: A militiaman with obviously little training poses boastfully with his FN rifle for the cameraman. The passenger is unimpressed or simply war weary, or both.

For some time friends of mine in Lourenço Marques had been talking of leaving. Portugal was the first choice but it was a costly move, the economy there was struggling and job prospects were poor. South Africa was the next. It was a short step away and to most Portuguese it seemed invincible under the National Party government, apartheid notwithstanding.

So they stayed, living on hope.

Late in 1973 I made another visit to northern Mozambique because I could feel something in the air, an intangible yet distinct sense of change. I went back to Mueda, the embattled village on the Mueda plateau about 50 kilometres south of the Tanzanian border, home of the fighting Maconde tribe. It was the most accessible and palpable part of Portugal's frontline. Here the will-o'-the-wisp war was easily visible every day.

Mueda was still under the same sluggish siege as before, with Frelimo sporadically tossing mortar bombs and 75mm shells from recoilless guns into the village, the troops firing randomly back and patrols venturing out in sandbag-laden Berliet trucks or on foot to hunt down the guerrillas, chasing moths in the dark.

The mood here was resignation – hang in until the tour of duty is over, pray a mortar doesn't land on you before then, get out as soon and as far as possible.

Mueda was small, a haphazard scattering of houses, matchbox trading stores and army barracks with an airfield on one side and on the other a crude collection of grass huts where prostitutes of all races worked. The roads were dirt tracks. Water came from a pump station outside the defended perimeter so it was regularly sabotaged by Frelimo. Consequently the largest cause of casualties was not Frelimo but hepatitis.

It was a dreary place, high and often cold and blanketed by cloud. When the ageing Nord Atlas transport I hitched a ride in landed the ground crew hastily shooed everyone out and unloaded fast so it could take off. The arrival of a plane frequently attracted bombs from Frelimo in the nearby bush.

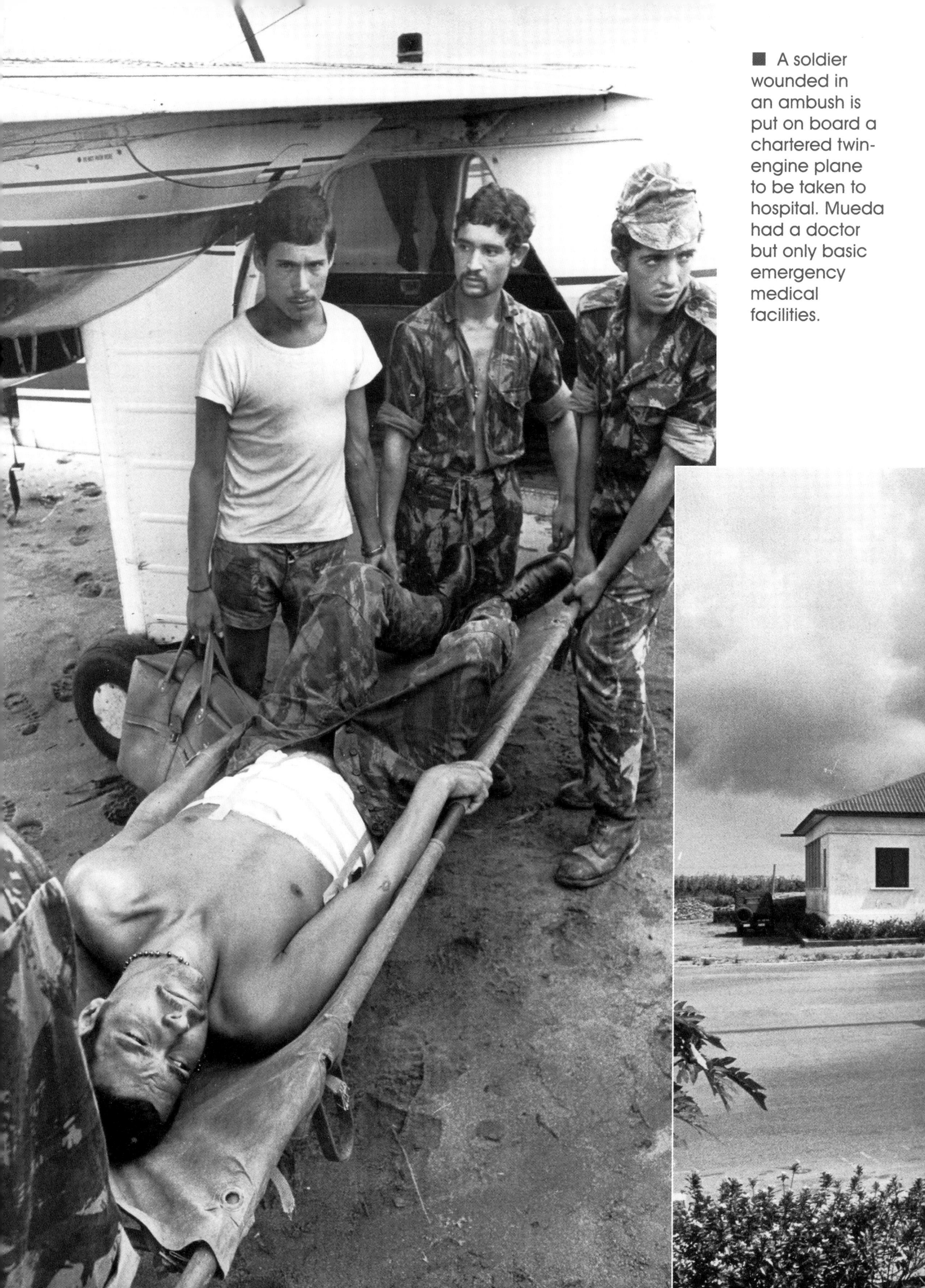

A soldier wounded in an ambush is put on board a chartered twin-engine plane to be taken to hospital. Mueda had a doctor but only basic emergency medical facilities.

"For some time friends of mine in Lourenço Marques had been talking of leaving ... they stayed, living on hope."

■ An Alouette III helicopter, the main workhorse of the Portuguese Air Force, comes into Mueda from a patrol. Some of these powerful French-built machines were equipped with 20mm cannons and were highly effective in hunting ground forces.

■ A Portuguese soldier shows an unexploded bomb and the remnants of others that landed on or near the Mueda airfield.

■ Mueda's only land link with the outer world was along tracks like this, where troops head a convoy going to fetch supplies. They are careful to walk on the tracks, which have been checked for mines by men prodding the sand with rods.

Mueda was, in fact, in stalemate and had been so for years. Neither side could win the dismal struggle in the middle of nowhere for a piece of territory anyone, except the Maconde, wanted nor cared for.

It was the whole Mozambique conflict in microcosm. Frelimo had absolutely no hope of winning militarily. It had neither the manpower nor the resources. Its lines of supply and reinforcement were already extremely long and overstretched.

Portuguese fears of their striking farther south were unfounded. They might indeed have arranged acts of sabotage but guerrilla attack was not on the cards. Moreover, some of the tribal areas they would have had to pass through were not particularly fond of Frelimo.

Both sides were thus holding the line as best they could, neither with the power to win outright.

Such was the overall scene on 25 April 1974 when a group of Portuguese generals toppled Portuguese President Américo Tomás and Prime Minister Marcello Caetano and set up a military junta.

It took took the world by surprise except for the very select few members of a small, highly secret cliqué among the military in Mozambique and, probably, in Angola.

The war was over, although not officially.

■ Troops bring back to base a shattered Berliet truck that detonated a landmine placed above an unexploded Portuguese aerial bomb.

But for a few diehards the entire Portuguese force in Mozambique heaved a gigantic sigh of relief, laid down their weapons (but kept them close at hand) and hoped Frelimo would do the same.

Right after the coup a multitude of political parties bloomed like spring flowers, covering just about every politiocal philosophy known to man and some that were not. The situation was further complicated by tribal divisions, a plunging economy and race friction.

Frelimo's initial response was to intensify its guerrilla attacks because it feared, naively, that as an ordinary political party it might not win a general election. If it had to negotiate, it would do so from a position of strength and the only strength it had was military. The Beira–Rhodesia corridor became more dangerous than ever with ambushes and train derailments.

Lisbon's response was to pump in more troops, none of whom was keen to risk life and limb in a conflict that seemed pointless. The local response was a surge of racism in Beira and Lourenço Marques.

In the looming Frelimo shadow, inter-party rivalry became violent with attempted assassinations, bombings and beatings, mostly by hard-core right-wingers. Whites had weak political clout in a population of 8.5 million blacks. More ominous was the influence of the tribalism that dissected the whole territory into distinct ethnic groups.

After the coup the Lisbon junta set up a civilian provisional government. When it proved unable to defuse tensions or introduce political reform fast enough it was replaced by a five-man junta headed by the governor-general.

The first breeze to stir the political doldrums came in August 1974, in Lourenço Marques. Black stevedores from the harbour demonstrated at the governor's 'palace' – a freedom they had not enjoyed for decades. They crammed the streets outside the gracious old colonial residence, loudly demanding a wage increase.

In August the Portuguese at last announced an official ceasefire. Fighting began slowing in the north. I flew north again and found that the war was about to end.

By then Frelimo had already capitalized on the Portuguese thirst for peace.

A Frelimo unit had broadcast a false ceasefire report and a couple of days later sent a message asking the commander of the Omar outpost on the northern border, a young lieutenant, to meet them to discuss terms. When the lieutenant arrived he and his 131 men were surrounded and surrendered.

There was no retaliation and no harm was done. The desire for peace was spreading so fast that an unofficial

■ Protesters crowd outside the gates of the governor's 'palace', blocking streets for hours while their womenfolk wait patiently on the sidewalk around the corner.

but genuine ceasefire emerged between the 10,000 or so Frelimo and 65,000-strong Portuguese army – just short of ten years after the war started.

The army dropped thousands of leaflets in the war zones showing photos of guerrillas and troops with their arms around each other in a bush camp somewhere. It explained that Portugal's old government had been overthrown.

"So why do you keep on fighting?" the leaflet asked, "Let us finish this war which brings disgrace, hunger and death. Let us be friends."

It worked. In the Cabo Delgado war zone, which included the hotspot Mueda, guerrillas bombarded a heavily fortified village just before they were themselves 'bombed' with leaflets. The next day they entered the village under a flag of truce.

Guerrillas began openly coming into towns and villages to buy supplies, window shop and talk to people in black suburbs. Along the ravaged Beira–Rhodesia corridor they approached white farmers via their labour, asking them not to quit the country. Some agreed, among them Afrikaners.

Troops were abandoning bush camps like that at Nangolo, close to Tanzania, where the war had started in 1964 with the killing of the priest. One company in Cabo Delgado detained their own colonel when he ordered them to fight.

Fraternization spread so fast it was beyond the control of the political leaders on both sides.

I flew to Tete, the crossing point on the Zambezi River established centuries ago, long before the Portuguese arrived, by Arab slavers and ivory traders. It was almost a home from home, so familiar had its eternal dust and sewage odours become.

There I met my first Frelimo, Raimundo Dalepa, commander of 253 guerrillas operating in the Tete district. A Portuguese captain I knew arranged a meeting in the home of an Indian trader in the town.

A few weeks earlier Dalepa would have shot us on sight. He was 27 and had been a guerrilla for almost ten years. A Maconde, he had operated in the Cabo Delgado area until four years previously when Frelimo sent him to lead the action around Tete.

He was a lean and rather cocky man wearing borrowed Portuguese camouflage fatigues and carrying an AK-47 plus a heavy Russian automatic pistol. He wore a small gold crucifix on a thin gold chain around his neck.

■ Men of Dalepa's unit at ease in the small kraal they occupied outside Tete. They are wearing new clothes given by locals to replace their tattered combat kit.

■ Raimundo Dalepa, leader of the Tete guerrillas in the Tete district, shows off his AK-47 after the fighting ended in Mozambique.

> "I know what I was fighting for and that was *uhuru*," he said through an interpreter.
> "And if *uhuru* is coming and the Portuguese are not fighting, how can I carry on fighting? Our wish is to work with Africans and all other colours together."

He told meetings of blacks and a sprinkling of whites that it was not Frelimo alone who won this war, but also the troops who overthrew the dictatorship in Lisbon.

Dalepa said he had killed a number of people but could not remember how many and seemed reluctant to discuss details. I was not going to press him for them and had to take into account that in these odd circumstances I had to treat his words with caution.

"Were the Portuguese good fighters, as good or better than Frelimo?" I asked.

"The world can judge," he said, "We had a very hard time in the bush. We had no food, no clothes, no shoes, only faith in victory. The Portuguese had cars and food and shoes, but ... I would rather die than be pushed off the pavement in my own country."

Yet I could not forget the dozens of children and women I saw minus legs and arms, or dead, because they had stepped on Frelimo landmines.

■ Dalepa's men pose for the picture in a grouping they would never have used in combat but there is no doubt they are experienced in bush fighting. Their AK-47s are well worn.

The frenetic politicking in the territory since the 25 April coup had not produced any viable alternative party or policy to Frelimo and the chances of that happening were receding as Frelimo's stocks rose.

The expectation was that after its months of rudderless confusion, Mozambique would soon have a coalition government formed by the local junta and Frelimo and thereafter a Frelimo-dominated government through elections.

The change of attitude between Portuguese forces and Frelimo since the ceasefire had been dramatic. The guerrillas' response to the army's overtures had become a flood. Frelimo's influence had risen sharply because it was no longer maintaining a pointless attack, it was being seen as the dominant movement and senior Frelimo commanders were publicly calling on whites to stay.

Whites in the war zones reacted positively. But not the majority of those in the cities of Beira and Lourenço Marques where the killing had not reached – perhaps because in the cities imagination was worse than the reality and the fear of ferocious black nationalist rule was keener.

It was difficult to see how people could live amicably with an ex-enemy who had destroyed by every possible means – indiscriminately killed innocents with landmines, murdered and massacred – but what was the alternative? The Portuguese were also guilty of horrors.

Hope began to rise. Euphoria spread. Maybe there was a future. And then, suddenly, the generals back in Lisbon broke their promise of consultation and elections. They decreed that Frelimo were the rightful rulers and Mozambique would be handed over to them in a few days, on 7 September, with the formal independence ceremony on 25 June the following year. The decision shocked all but a few of the Portuguese in the country and also some blacks. Everything came crashing down.

War erupted again in Mozambique, but this time only in Lourenço Marques with minor reflection in Beira. It was the largely forgotten, quite bloody and bizarre One-Week War.

Resentment there had been simmering for weeks, aggravated by the fraternization between Frelimo and Portuguese troops. The great majority of Portuguese in the city was conservative, embittered by the war, influenced by the policy of neighbouing South Africa and with little faith in black ability.

When, after the Lisbon junta's arbitrary decision, pro-Frelimo liberals in the city began celebrating; the white temper rose to boiling point. Young people – whites, blacks and mixed – drove the streets waving Frelimo flags from car windows. Noisy meetings were held. It was the strangest conflict I have experienced – drive a few kilometres to watch confrontation, bloodshed and

■ One of my photographers, Ruphin Coudyzer, happened to be ambling toward the *Noticias* building, where we had an office, when he came across the rioters and took this picture. They wanted to beat him up but when he said he was a Belgian tourist, they brushed off his clothes, patted him on the shoulder and sent him on his way.

destruction – drive back into the lap of five-star luxury, then out again, and so on, and on. A big Frelimo rally was held on Friday 6 September. Frelimo supporters going to the big Machava stadium on the outskirts of LM were in no mood to brook interference; a white man with more bravura than brains got himself beaten to death by blacks when he tried to stop them.

By mid-afternoon more than 30,000 people were crammed into it in a state of high political intoxication. They sang anthems, waved flags and banners and displayed huge posters of Samora Machel.

The trouble began back in town. It is an unusual experience to see revolution bud as an incident and flower into mayhem. I was drinking coffee in the Avenida Republica in downtown LM late afternoon. The atmosphere was trigger-taut. Hardly anyone was working. The sidewalk cafés, restaurants and bars were filled with Portuguese, mostly men. The subject on every tongue was the Frelimo takeover.

■ I moved to the rooftop of the nearby Tivoli Hotel and from there captured this scene of the angry mob smashing the windows of the main city newspaper, *Noticias*, and trashing its vehicles. *Noticias* had almost overnight turned pro-Frelimo.

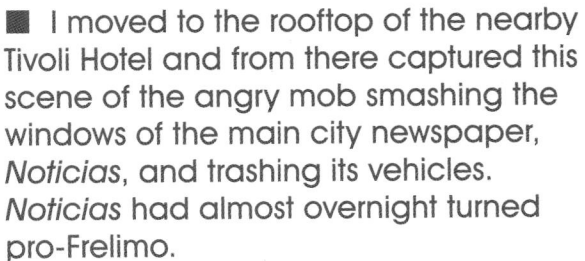

Streams of cars and trucks passed by, some flying Frelimo flags. A small saloon car came slowly past full of noisy white students exuberantly waving large Frelimo banners from all the windows and shouting slogans.

It was too much for one young soldier at a café. He pulled off his belt, charged the car and swung the buckle to shatter the windscreen.

The car jerked to a stop. In seconds a wave of shirt-sleeved men rose from sidewalk tables and ran to it, all restraint snapped by the spark of violence. More rushed from the other side of the street. The car and students were surrounded by a bloodthirsty mob seeking outlet for their rage.

They smashed the windows and toppled the car on its side with the terrified students still in it. I was there next, shooting with my Leica. The crowd began yelling at me – the Press was not popular.

■ Above: Portuguese infuriated by the pro-Frelimo demonstrations in Lourenço Marques turned on me when I tried to take pictures of them and the carload of students they had just overturned in the Avenida Republica. Two of them tried to block my camera lens. The one with his face obscured is a policeman. They backed off when they heard my South African accent.

■ Left: We did not ask for it but the Portuguese military decided foreign journalists needed some protection from the anti-Frelimo troublemakers, in our office in the *Noticias* building. The man with the G3 got bored after a couple of days and vanished. Beyond him are reporter Tom Roy, at the telex, and photographer Ruphin Coudyzer.

■ Far right: Several thousand Portuguese men and women gathered in the city's central plaza to protest the handover of the country to Frelimo. "This is Portugal," was their main theme and FICO was one of the many right-wing groups staking claims to rule. Many whites were out of work with the economy grinding slow in the post-coup hiatus, or simply stayed away.

That night the pent-up tensions exploded into widespread violence. Exuberant mobs of Frelimo supporters in the black *bairros* (suburbs) that almost surrounded the city's landward side roamed the streets stoning cars and traders' shops.

Mobs of hysterical anti-Frelimo protesters smashed windows and threw petrol bombs into the offices of a magazine and a liberal politician – who had already survived an assassination attempt – and plunged suburbs into chaos. About a hundred people raided a hostel and offices near the university, whose students were prominently pro-Frelimo. They methodically smashed plate-glass windows while soldiers and police watched, then went inside. When everything was wrecked, the police made them leave. There was no doubt whose side they were on.

A dim-witted student shouted, "Long live Frelimo!" The mob descended on him with chairs from a nearby sidewalk café and would have killed him had a passing army patrol not rescued him.

Some of the mob grabbed the barrels of their automatic rifles and tried to wrest them away. They stopped when the soldiers cocked their weapons with ominous clicks.

In the dead of that night some clever rebels managed to elude troops guarding an ammunition dump outside LM and set it on fire. It blew up with a thump felt all over the city.

The next morning noisy cavalcades of cars filled with yelling young right-wingers waving Portuguese flags, led by motorcycles and buzzbikes with horns blaring, paraded the streets of downtown LM.

Truckloads of blacks flaunting Frelimo banners passed them going to the Machava stadium for another mass gathering. White men leaped from their cars and tried to rip away the Frelimo flags. The confrontation was about to erupt into violence when traffic police, of all people, stopped it by moving the vehicles on.

The city was grinding to a halt. Water and electricity stopped when gangs stoned city vehicles in the *bairros*. A general strike by black workers shut down the remaining services and shops. Most whites stayed at home or settled down in a few cafés open for business to watch the fun, but tempers were fraying.

The handover to end four centuries of Portuguese rule was supposed to be at midnight that night. It had no visible effect. After dark trouble spread. In Beira a grenade was tossed into a bank and angry crowds roamed the streets.

In LM a large crowd smashed into the civil prison in the Polana suburb to free about 200 members of the former Portuguese political police who were arrested after the coup.

It was a strange sight. About a thousand spectators – men, women and children – watched in the pleasant, leafy suburb as the mob leaders tried to talk soldiers into releasing the men. To distract the guards the crowd battered and overturned the prison commissioner's car parked outside and threatened to set the whole prison alight. To back their threat they drove up a large truck and aimed it at the main door.

Some of the crowd smashed open a side door and burst into the prison. Confronting them were rows of soldiers armed with automatic weapons. Here was the recipe for massacre.

It did not happen because people in the mob happily hugged the soldiers and told them, "You can't shoot us, we are also Portuguese."

The security policemen fled, most to South Africa where many were taken into the South Africa Security Police and various Defence Force units.

■ Above: Crowds gather to listen to speeches from a balcony in downtown Lourenço Marques from which hangs a crude banner proclaiming: The Square of Liberated Mozambique. The protestors are demanding that Mozambique remain part of Portugal.

■ Exuberant anti-Frelimo demonstrators roamed the city streets waving the Portuguese flag and chanting, "This is Portugal!" in vehicles and on foot.

■ At this early stage the downtown demonstrations were still relatively peaceful, more sound than fury, and kept the onlookers entertained as they paraded the streets.

■ Above: What the protestors did not know was that while all this was happening, the authorities released other prisoners from the jail. There was zero chance of their ever appearing in court.

■ Right: Spectators and police look on as young folk opposing Frelimo wave the flag in the Avenida Republica.

■ An admiring young Portuguese woman waves one of the scores of flags brought on to the streets (above). Behind her, and facing, is an impromptu cavalcade of motorcyclists.

Sunday 8 September saw the haphazard rebellion begin to gell. A collection of right-wingers formed the Movement of Free Mozambique (MFM) and produced their own flag, a concoction of Mozambican and Portuguese symbols.

They seized the large *Radio Clube de Moçambique* building in the city centre and made it their headquarters, broadcasting a stream of appeals in Portuguese, English and African languages for support. Volunteers, armed with a motley assortment of guns, self-importantly stood sentry at doors and windows and on the roof.

■ A happy member of the rebel Movement for Free Moçambique flaunts a mocked-up new flag for the country from the *Radio Clube* balcony for cheering crowds below.

■ The rebels posted guards, apparently defectors from the Portuguese forces, on top of the *Radio Clube* building.

44

■ A rebel in home-made kit of camouflage uniform with a motorcycle helmet and shotgun yells at the crowd below.

■ Some of the rebels were seriously armed, like this MFM supporter with an AK-47.

■ Atop the *Radio Clube* building.

WATERSHED

■ Others, though armed, demonstrated peaceful intent by using the barrels of their shotguns as flower vases, emulating the troops who carried the coup in Lisbon.

■ Above: The victory symbol is repeated from a smashed *Radio Clube* window by a rebel occupying it.

■ Above right: A joyous Portuguese father and family celebrate the anti-Frelimo uprising with two raised fingers for victory.

■ Right: Portuguese forces did nothing to stop the rebellion at this stage, but cautiously placed soldiers in armoured personnel carriers in streets near the *Clube*.

WATERSHED

■ A couple of days later the crowd outside the *Radio Clube* went into raptures when a senior civil police officer, a Colonel Tavares, arrived at the *Clube*, thinking he had come to give support to the rebel movement. They exuberantly hugged him and a colleague. In fact he had come to persuade the rebels to leave the *Clube*. As he was leaving, they heard of this and their joy turned instantly to anger. They began to rock his car and might have done him serious injury had he not suddenly put his foot down and sped away.

It was another day of noisy parades and motorcades. Samora Machel warned that if the Portuguese did not squash the MFM, Frelimo would resume the guerrilla war.

The Portuguese took the threat seriously. In Beira they sent heavily armed military police into town to disperse 2,000 mainly white demonstrators with teargas. A black policeman was badly hurt when a grenade exploded on his chest.

Back in LM happy crowds celebrated outside the *Radio Clube*. Inside I found a bedlam of waving arms and loud voices as dozens of politicians fought, pleaded and argued for places in power. Taking pictures was banned – no one wanted to be identified later.

Outside they turned the city centre's numerous heroic monuments into platforms to watch the action and display home-made banners lauding the rebellion.

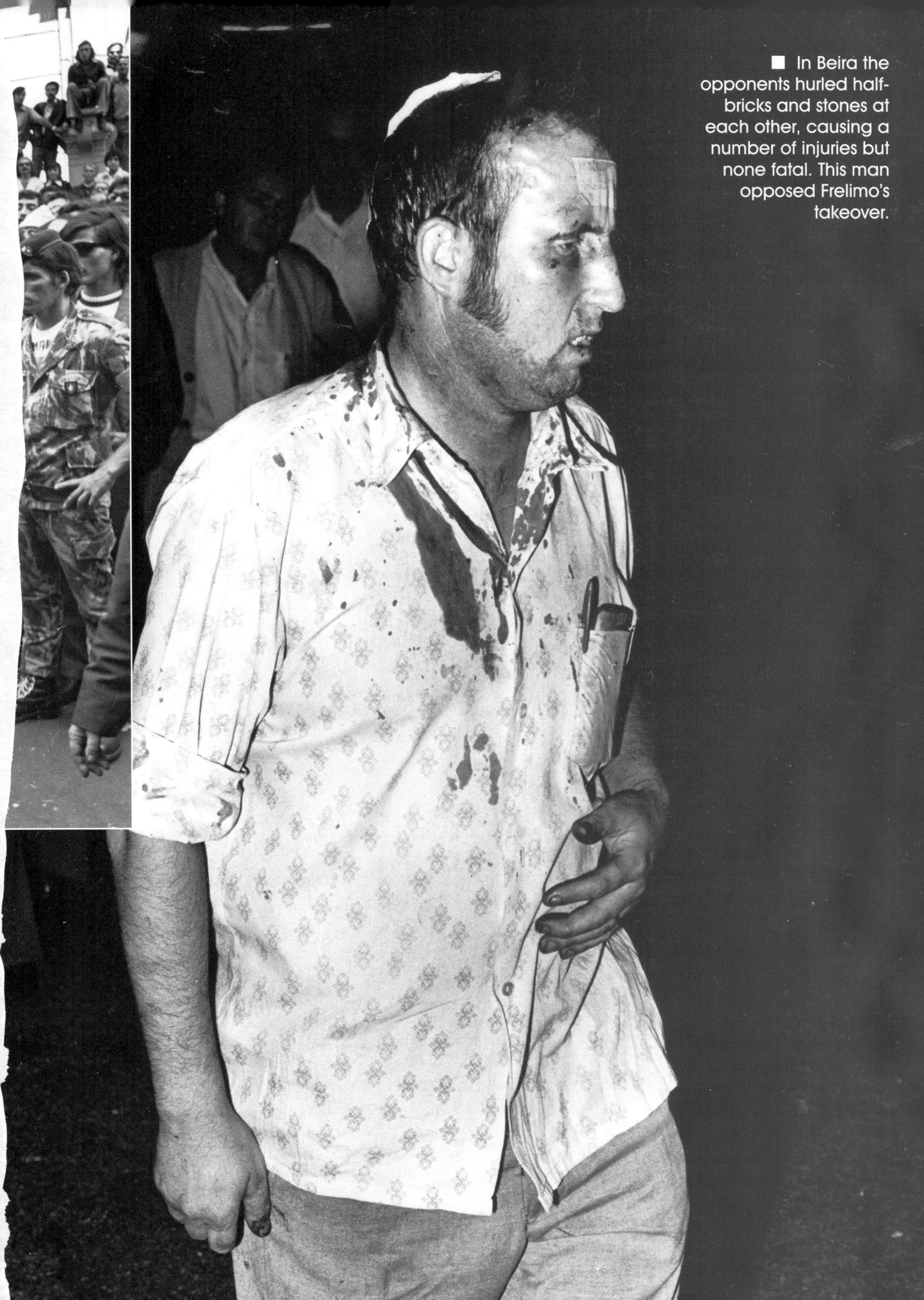

In Beira the opponents hurled half-bricks and stones at each other, causing a number of injuries but none fatal. This man opposed Frelimo's takeover.

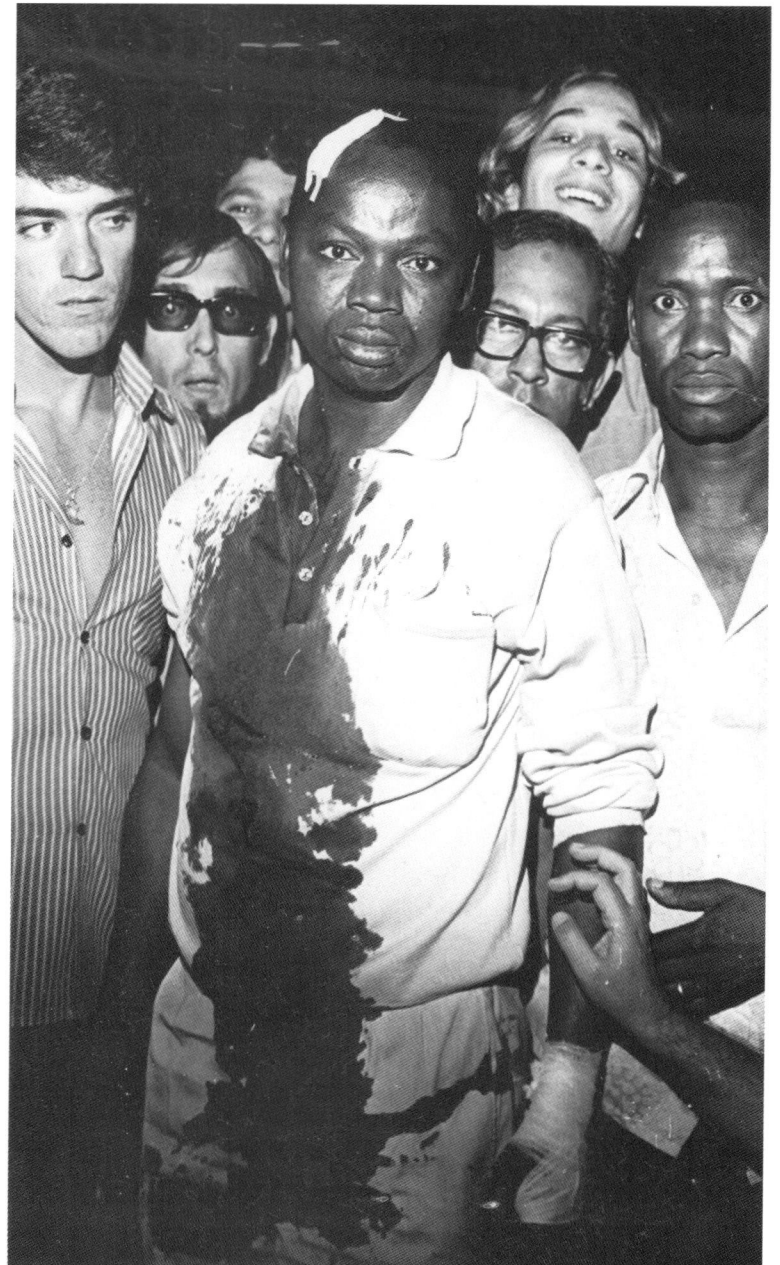

■ Above: A number of injuries, but no fatalities, resulted from the clashes in Beira. There were no clear racial divisions, just those who opposed Frelimo and those who did not.

■ Top right: The clashes between pro- and anti-Frelimo mobs in Beira were serious but brief. Here a Portuguese woman and a man shout the odds at each other, though it is not clear who supports what.

■ Above right: The fighting stopped when troops were sent in after Frelimo threatened to resume the war. No one expected the troops to shoot their fellow citizens, however.

In the tin shanties and grass huts of the *bairros* on the city outskirts the black population was ominously quiet early on Sunday. We tried to go in but, perhaps fortunately, it was not possible because the Portuguese police and troops were not cooperative.

The road to the airport was open, however. Travellers had been driving the few kilometres between airport and city through the Xipamanine/ Lagoa area, known as Grasstown. We had gone back and forth several times to send film to Johannesburg.

I hired one of the few taxis still doing business and asked the driver to take me and Tom Roy via a familiar back route through a small industrial area parallel to the main airport road. He was a fat, phlegmatic middle-aged Portuguese wearing the usual floppy peaked cap.

The back route was strangely still. Not a soul in sight. All the warehouses and workshops were closed. Half a dozen overturned trucks and cars lay beside the street, some burned out. It looked abandoned, quieter than it should be even on a Sunday. The driver heaved a sigh of relief when we reached the airport where a plane was about to leave.

In the parking area a convoy was forming up, a motley collection of

■ Protestors turned the city centres' numerous heroic monuments into platforms from which to watch the action and display home-made banners lauding the rebellion.

cars and large and small trucks. Civilians armed with an assortment of firearms, from pistols to rifles and shotguns, rode on the truck platforms. No one could say what was going on, only that the convoy was heading for the city.

"Why now, suddenly?"

Shrugs.

The cabbie was getting nervous. The choice was to stay at the airport indefinitely or join the convoy into town. We tagged along with one or two cars behind us. Just in front of us was a large truck with high side walls. A dozen or more men stood in the back.

We moved off at the slow pace set by the lead vehicle, forcing the cabbie to travel in second or third gear. Out of the car park the tarred road narrowed and the reed-and-thatch huts and palms of Grasstown jostled close.

At first there were few signs of life but as we moved deeper into Grasstown more and more black people began appearing on both sides, twenty to thirty metres away – men, women and children – shouting and waving fists at the convoy. Men on the trucks waved flags and shouted insults back.

A few stones sailed through the air toward us.

The men on the lorry ahead reacted instantly. Long barrels suddenly appeared above the side walls. There was a sharp crackle of rifle fire and the deep thud of shotgun blasts. The people melted away into the long grass and crowded huts.

The cabbie went into panic mode. He yelled and gesticulated in anger. He glared at us accusingly, face blotched with fear. He pounded the steering wheel. There was not a thing he could do. He dared not leave the convoy, which was occupying the centre of the road. Tom, too, was looking anxious. I saw his eyes widen like saucers at something ahead and glanced up.

A couple of corpses lay at the roadside, one was a man lying flat on his back, the toes of his shoes pointing skyward, arms at his sides, his head pulped to mush by chunks of concrete lying beside him, blood spreading in a large pool. The other was equally battered.

As we slowly passed about two metres away, the driver screamed Portuguese imprecations.

The journey could not have lasted more than ten to 15 minutes. With the adrenalin rush it seemed to zoom by in seconds. When we reached the end, where Grasstown ended and the city began, there was a small police post, and our cab jerked to a stop. The cabbie flung open the rear doors and shouted "Go! Go!"

He did not wait for his money. The old taxi clattered away probably faster than it had ever travelled before.

The convoy was of over-exuberant rebels driving celebratory cavalcades between airport and city and picking off blacks like clay pigeons. It was like poking a stick into a hornets' nest.

Blacks erupted from the huts and shanties falling on one passing parade, pelting the vehicles with a hail of stones, dragged out some drivers and beat them up, killing three.

The most bizarre feature of the One-Week War was how little it affected the lives of the city's glitterati and the rather few tourists who had ventured to Mozambique, of course not expecting upheaval.

Business at the famed Polana Hotel, one of Africa's most gracious and luxurious hostelries, carried on as usual, serving superb meals and fine wines from its voluminous cellars. Other city-centre hotels like the Cardoso and Tivoli did the same.

U-shaped, the Polana's widespread wings of luxurious rooms embraced a broad lawn and ornate swimming pool overlooking Delagoa Bay. The central section housed

■ On the outskirts of the city on the way to the airport is evidence of the eruption of anger in the black townships. On this road a Portuguese man lies dead (above) and a smashed and burned truck lies abandoned on the roadside (below right). Another victim has had his head smashed in, killed by angry Africans (far right).

Conversely, life for the rich goes on, unchanged and oblivious. The Polana Hotel is renowned for its lunches on the lawn where flocks of waiters serve exotic seafood dishes prepared by master chefs while only a couple of kilometres away angry, brutal killing is in progress. The nearby fighting did not stop the young ladies of LM from making frequent use of the big Polana swimming pool close to the luncheon tables. Nor were places like Quitexe, a popular resort north of LM, affected by the conflict there or in Beira. Is it possible that the tourists didn't know it was happening? Or did they just not care?

a big, airy, sunlit foyer and lounge floored in colourful mosaic plus intimate bar, dining rooms and patio. Service was immaculate, the cuisine excellent, the wine list exhaustive. This was the social hub of LM, always lively, always buzzing with the city's elite and wealthy visitors.

It made the war a uniquely different scene to cover for foreign correspondents. A leisurely breakfast of scrambled eggs and smoked salmon. A taxi downtown to watch the demos and to the city edge to see who was shooting whom. Back to the Polana for salted dogs – half fill a tall glass with crushed ice, sprinkle a liberal dash of salt on it, pour on a decent tot of good gin and top up with fresh grapefruit juice. Invigorating – and a large lunch of magnificent prawns washed down with white wine. Then to the city centre again and back in time for sundowners before a five-course dinner. There was no point in venturing forth at night, one could not enter the *bairros* without getting killed.

News of the upheaval brought a herd of foreign correspondents. The locals did not like it. A TV cameraman was punched. A photographer was threatened by angry whites who backed off when they learned he was South African – the Portuguese right-wingers all assumed South Africa was backing them.

Most came by air or road and one by train from the border. He complained that when the train broke down he had to help push it, a first for a British hack going to war.

Those coming by road had to run a gauntlet of blacks enraged by the actions of the whites in LM. Some were stopped by mobs armed with clubs and pangas who banged on the roofs of their cars and made them get out, stole their cigarettes and whisky and reluctantly let them go when they identified themselves as British.

At a roadblock one watched a black man beside the car sharpening the blade of a large panga on the tarmac. The man glanced up and grinned evilly at him as if he was next on the menu. They saw shops being plundered and fired and a burning car with two dead people in it, presumably white.

Liquor consumption at the Polana soared that evening.

■ There was no mistaking the intent of the men at the roadblocks with so much evidence of their handiwork cluttering the median.

■ All roads into LM passed through blue-collar or black suburbs. Anyone entering the city during the rebellion had to run a gauntlet of impromptu roadblocks manned by Frelimo supporters. They all had to pass a test: when they were shown two raised fingers, as the black man in front is doing here, they had to make the choice – one or two. One finger meant one government for Mozambique: Frelimo. Two meant you supported two governments, Frelimo and the rebels, and invited a beating and possibly death. Some travellers thought the two fingers was a victory sign, and suffered. This white driver here was forewarned, or chose to take the advice of the other African next to the VW.

■ This café has been trashed by rebels because it was used by left-wing students.

On Monday 9 September soldiers made safe the airport route.

It was anybody's guess how long the uprising would last although it was patently doomed to fail. Frelimo was hugely supported in the LM region although it did not yet have military muscle there.

In South Africa hard-core Nationalists were urging the government to support the rebels and so fulfil the old Transvaal Republic's ambition of controlling LM. Rumours were widespread that defence minister P. W. Botha had moved army units close to the border.

By Tuesday, the *Radio Clube* had become the main gathering place for rebel supporters. The street outside was filled with up to 10,000 cheering men, women and children.

Then came the crunch: a broadcast by the MFM announcing they were handing over the *Radio Clube* to the civil police.

As the stunning news poured from radios the mood outside changed to anger. Minutes later paratroops backed by armoured vehicles moved slowly up the street. They were stopped by a mob of people yelling insults and calls of "Traitor!" A sky-shouter plane circled low telling people to go home.

Suddenly several thunderous blasts shook the air, almost deafening us. They were percussion bombs – thunderflashes – dropped by paratroops from the building to scare away the crowd.

It worked. Most fled like rabbits, urged on by a flurry of shots fired into the air from automatic weapons.

They almost bowled us over and we too fled, albeit just around the corner.

The MFM began leaving the building. Most went unobtrusively through a back door. They abandoned an assortment of hastily acquired weapons from shotguns to heavy machine guns and grenades. Women wept.

"This is not the end, my friend, it is only the beginning," an MFM chief told me as he departed.

He was half right. The violence was spreading.

The tension was almost tangible and the danger of a backlash very real. Luckily the army kept their cool. Had just one shot been fired by troops or the MFM, the scene could have turned into a bloodbath.

It was impossible to get into the black areas without the probability of getting killed so we could not personally check conditions there. But there was action aplenty.

Portuguese Air Force men under a Colonel Cardoso led a charge by 300 men from their base on the other side of the airport runway to recapture the terminal and control tower. There was some gunfire in which an MFM man was hit and an unfortunate passenger was accidentally

shot as he arrived from Beira. He died in hospital.

All commercial flights to and from South Africa were stopped. Residents in the *bairros* blocked the airport road with tree trunks and stones but let African buses through.

Word trickled in about vigilantes hunting blacks in the *bairros*.

Crazily, in much of downtown LM life began to look almost normal. Some shops, sidewalk cafés and restaurants had reopened.

It was a crazy week. We rushed around gathering information, getting to hotspots, interviewing rebels and Frelimos. In between we relaxed at sidewalk cafés with coffee and Constantino brandy. Some evenings we dined at a tiny restaurant which served delicious prawns piri-piri on yellow rice.

It was a comfortable little war.

It peaked on the Tuesday night and early Wednesday amid a flurry of alarms, the beginnings of a panicky

■ With the erratic publication and distribution of newspapers, townsfolk try to keep up to date with events by reading pages posted on an easel outside a bank. In spite of Frelimo being mostly black and those against it mostly white, there was little obvious friction between the two races in downtown LM, away from the front-line friction.

flight of civilians from the city and the first grim tally of casualties.

An official announcement said about a hundred people had been killed or wounded. The total was certainly higher: more than a hundred wounded had been treated at the city hospital alone.

Soldiers chased us away when we tried to get into the hospital where the wounded were lying on the floor because all beds were occupied. A doctor said the hospital morgue was crammed.

Troops were struggling to contain mobs of Africans rampaging through the outer suburbs and threatening to spill into the city centre. The city shut up shop again when rumours spread that pro-Frelimos were planning a mass march of about 2,500 into the centre. White anxiety ran high. Strong forces of police and army, backed by armoured cars, sealed off the entrances to shantytowns.

Sporadic rifle and machine-gun fire and heavy explosions came from inside the townships. Escaping traders said all the schools and shops had been ransacked and destroyed and houses and vehicles burned. Some lost all they owned. Troops had fired shots in the air to scare off looters. Debris and the hulks of cars and trucks littered the roads.

An army major said the violence was not political: "They are just in a wild mood and completely out of hand."

I wondered what constituted the borderline between "wild" and "political" in Africa.

A band of black people marched toward the posh Polana suburb after a vigilante shot dead a black woman. Police and troops, supported by an armoured car blocked the road. They warned white onlookers to go away or risk being shot.

I sent a reporter, Deon du Plessis, and a photographer to check. They found the marchers and security forces gone. The roadblocks of rocks and heavy stones had been dismantled. Deon drove a little farther until a crowd of blacks materialized from nowhere. He stopped.

A young man offered to escort them in exchange for cigarettes. He warned: "If you see a crowd, give the one-finger Frelimo salute. A two-fingered salute will mean trouble."

A little farther a much larger crowd barred the road. One man brandished an axe. They milled around the car as it was searched. Their leader warned them not to go on, they would be dead already had they been Portuguese, he said.

They turned around in a hurry and then came the shock: all the dismantled roadblocks had been rebuilt. If they had been forced to flee they would have been trapped.

Not a soul was in sight, no troops, no blacks.

Deon, a strong man, hastily got out of the car and heaved aside enough boulders for them to drive through. No one appeared, no one tried to stop them. They could feel the hair rising on the backs of their necks.

That night Joaquim Chissano, deputy to Machel, broadcast an appeal for calm, aimed especially at blacks. He added a warning to Portuguese hotheads that they were outnumbered.

Next day, 11 September, the violence continued. A senior police officer emerged from the townships, still shaking from shock and fatigue, to announce that the toll of killed, stabbed and beaten had risen to two hundred.

Three other events marked that day. One was the arrival of the first Portuguese High Commissioner, Rear Admiral Victor Crespo. Few diplomats have begun their assignments in more difficult circumstances.

The second was the arrival in two frigates and by plane of Portuguese troops. By now the army was pretty much in control of most of the city. Casualty figures fluctuated wildly. No one will ever know how many bodies were left in unmarked graves in the urban jungle.

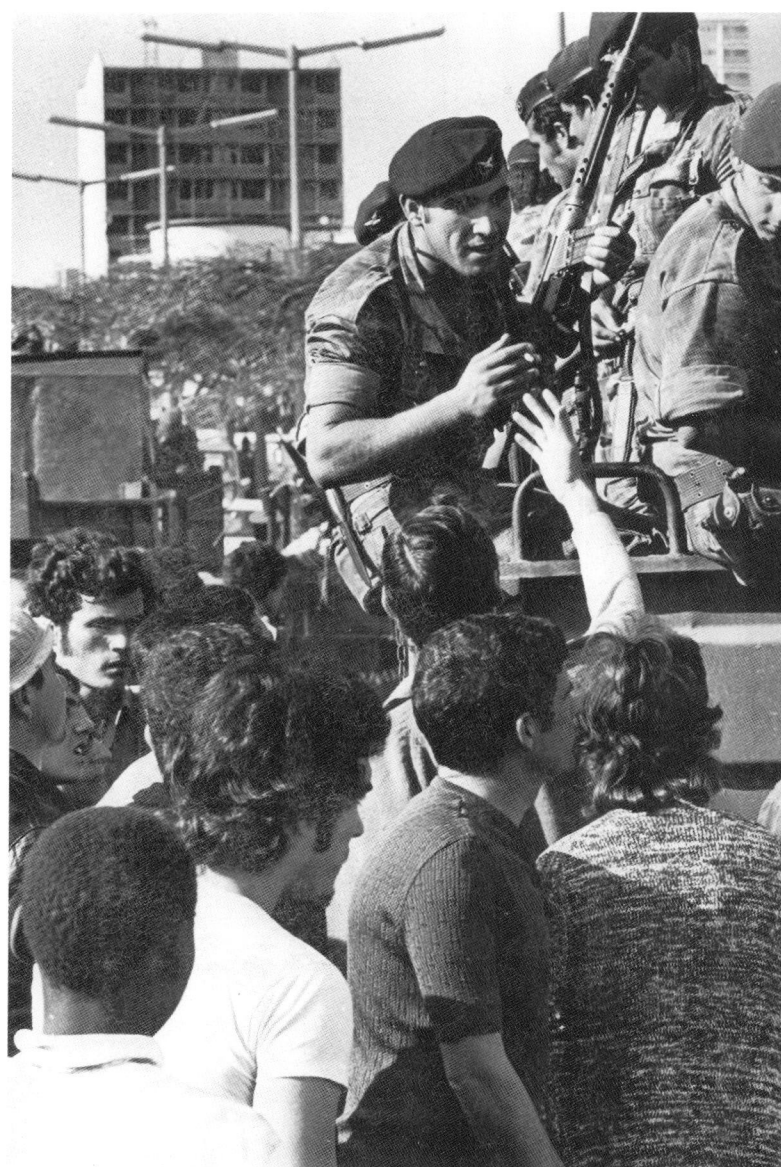

■ Left: The Portuguese army suddenly became very visible all over the city. Some of them, like this paratrooper, look like characters from a Rambo movie.

■ Above: In spite of the insults they hurled at the troops when the occupation of the *Radio Clube* was ended, the city folk remained on good terms with them. They were, after all, all Portuguese and the troops had been defending them against Frelimo attack for ten years. Here troops and civilians exchange chat and cigarettes in a city street.

■ Left: In Beira crowds welcome the arrival of soldiers while the civil police keep an eye on them.

■ Above top: A civil police Land Rover leads a Unimog with Portuguese troops on an LM street.

■ Above centre: Soldiers take their ease at an empty sidewalk café, one of many which closed during the rebellion.

■ Above: Others take a nap wherever they can find a place, in this case a corridor in the *Noticias* building.

The third event was a trick borrowed by the authorities from the old guard dictators: censorship. They cut all telecommunication links from LM to the world. Phones were dead. Telexes could not link with any others. The city became an information island.

It sent the large force of foreign correspondents into a major flap. How could they justify their existence, and their expenses? Eventually they chose one of their number to carry all their copy to South Africa and there file it to the various destinations. It meant a long and dangerous trip through the townships and roadblocks but it worked, although it made all their reports late.

My team was saved by the man staffing our bureau in Salisbury, Rhodesia. Our dead telex suddenly clattered into life with a message from him: we could file our copy via a link he had set up with the post office in Beira.

The link, I learned later, was one of his amorous conquests in the post office there. When he heard of the blackout he contacted her by phone because Beira had not been cut off entirely.

Never have so many owed so much to one affair. It gave us a full day's start on all the other media, to their huge envy.

On Thursday 12 September tension began to ease as both sides ran out of steam: hunger and the Portuguese forces tightened their grip. The authorities lifted the censorship and our phone and direct telex lines came back to life.

By Friday the One-Week War was all over bar the shouting. Remonstration replaced demonstration. To put the final nail in the coffin of rebel hopes an East African Airways plane arrived from Nairobi with 70 Frelimo troops – the first tangible, visible mark of the Frelimo takeover. Soon after came another Portuguese frigate loaded this time with Frelimos, making 200 in all. They carried well-worn AK-47s.

■ Above: This Frelimo man is clearly enjoying the limelight of the capital city they had been trying to reach and conquer for so many years. He is a militia man or auxiliary armed with an old model rifle.

■ Left: The Portuguese frigate *Jacinto Candido* docks in LM with a company of Frelimo brought from Beira. Here was the nightmare of most Mozambican whites come to life: the hated and feared Frelimo guerrillas, the perpetrators of atrocities, the vanguard of black nationalism, taking over their country and property.

■ This man in the Eastern Bloc helmet, probably also an auxiliary, has a rifle but his expression looks far deadlier.

The guerrillas were obviously under strict orders to behave and not to provoke. They maintained their presence in the streets, diplomatically outside the city centre – used mostly by whites – followed by small bands of hero-worshipping children.

Admiral Crespo held his first news conference. There would be no reprisals, he promised. Combined Frelimo and Portuguese patrols were keeping the peace.

But the exodus of whites had begun. It was led by seven leading former secret police officers and their families who were flown back to Portugal from Beira in an air force transport. At least one never made it: Francisco 'Frank the Ugly' Langa or 'The Butcher of Machava', one of the most feared interrogators, was caught and killed by rioters.

There were some quirky final touches. Daniel Roxo, the militant spokesman for the MFM, blew himself up with a hand grenade. Carlos 'Ginger Joe' Rocha, a well-known criminal who had escaped from prison, gave himself up. Life in the new Mozambique was not quite as nice as in prison, he said.

Nothing had changed at the Polana Hotel yet, except its guests. Seated at the next table at our last lunch were a large, fat, dark-complexioned man in a badly cut, three-piece black suit that looked bullet-proof, a large, fat, dark-complexioned woman in a similar suit and a six-o'clock shadow matching her husband's, and two children who could have been cloned from them. They said little and we could not understand a word.

They were Bulgarians. The Soviet bloc had sent him to teach the Mozambicans how to grow, of all things, maize.

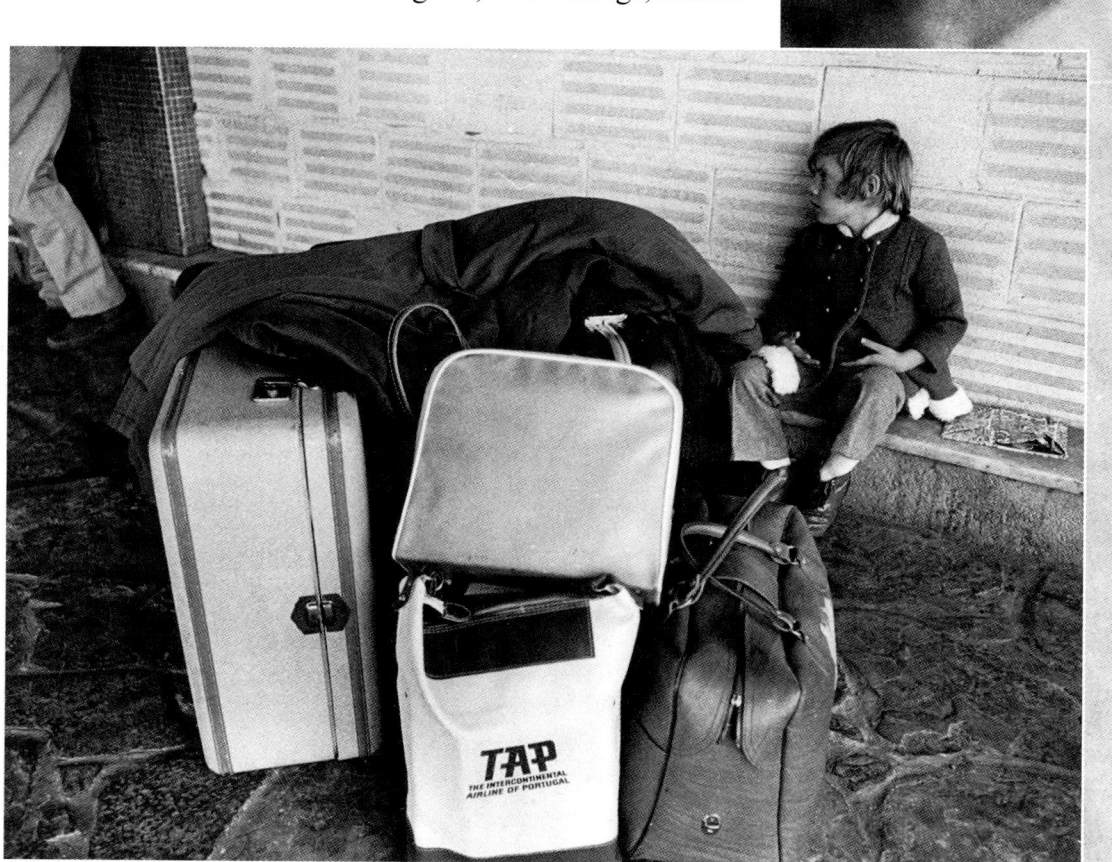

■ At the airport a boy keeps an eye on the family luggage while waiting to embark. Many Portuguese left most of their possessions behind, soon to be ransacked by Africans moving into the nearly empty suburbs.

■ A refugee displays the passport that will take him to a new and as yet unknown life elsewhere.

WATERSHED

"Combined Frelimo and Portuguese patrols were keeping the peace. But the exodus of whites had begun."

■ Far left: Soldiers help a Portuguese man quitting Mozambique load as many of his possessions as he can onto his truck before he heads for the Ressano Garcia/Komatipoort border post with South Africa. Most of an estimated 250,000 left within a week or two, most of them by road, the rest by air.

■ Above left: Every morning from about seven o'clock a pathetic procession form up in a side road near the Lourenço Marques military hospital: fifty to 60 cars of all kinds and conditions, some trucks and caravans, are all crammed with possessions from furniture to tricycles. Their owners and their families stand about near their vehicles talking gloomily of the life they are leaving and the unknown they are going to. They are waiting for the daily Portuguese army escort to the nearby Ressano Garcia/Komatipoort border to see them safely through the several roadblocks Frelimo have mounted. Otherwise the Frelimo soldiers will harass them and search their possessions. The same is happening in Beira, with convoys travelling to the Rhodesian border.

■ Left: Not all refugees are Portuguese whites. This man is leaving the restive city to return to his home village.

The decline of Mozambique was a sobering experience, more chilling than the violence. Within weeks after the September rebellion the entire country was bankrupt and disintegrating. Not even the former Belgian Congo had decayed so fast.

The collapse began with the transfer of Mozambique from Lisbon's rule to an interim Frelimo government pending full independence in 1975. The white exodus grew into a flood in spite of a plea by the youthful new premier, Joaquim Chissano, for them to stay.

They ignored him. They complained that they could not take money with them, they could not sell their homes and that work had dried up since the economy fell apart.

Thousands left every week. Long queues lined up daily at the South African consulate-general for visitor or transit visas. Many moved on to Portugal or Brazil, most stayed in South Africa, where a substantial community grew in Johannesburg.

In a short time the vast majority of the nearly quarter million Portuguese in Mozambique had departed.

Their going glaringly highlighted Lisbon's awful neglect, for four centuries, of this huge colony. It had never developed beyond a simple agrarian economy with 'pack, wrap and ship' services to neighbouring South Africa and Rhodesia. Even before the Portuguese coup it was severely stressed by the financial demands of Lisbon, falling exports, too much credit, rising living costs, a growing deficit and maladministration.

Just before the Lisbon coup the Mozambique authorities had anticipated foreign exchange earnings for 1974 of R450 million – a lot of money then. By the end of June they were a meagre R164 million. By the end of July the country's deficit had soared thanks to the huge confusion of successive, bewildered and hopelessly inefficient regimes the Lisbon junta installed in Mozambique. And then came the September rebellion.

These ills had been compounded by rampant corruption as officials and businessmen tried to milk the country for as much as they could before Frelimo took over.

Lisbon had done little or nothing to train blacks into the economy past the agricultural and manual labour levels. Most of the fragile infrastructure ground to a stop with the exodus of whites. Tourism evaporated overnight when the trouble began.

The Polana Hotel became a kind of social and economic barometer. In its heyday it ranked with Cairo's Shepheard's, Singapore's Raffles, Cape Town's Mount Nelson, Nairobi's Norfolk and Rhodesia's Victoria Falls.

Within weeks it was a starved shadow of its former self. The visitors and most of the local elite were gone. The bar was fast running out of the extraordinary variety. Even

■ An overjoyed President Samora Machel in his fatigues, with his deputy Joaquim Chissano on his left in a suit, greets the Chinese delegation at the airport. Behind him to his right, partly obscured, is Portugal's governor in Mozambique, Vice Admiral Victor Crespo.

beer was in short supply. Breakfast was one egg, if you were lucky, a small piece of bacon if you were luckier, and maybe a rather stale bread roll. Lunch was soup of unknown origin, depending on the chef's ingenuity. Or perhaps chicken and rice. Dinner the same. Gone was the magnificent patio buffet resplendent with seafoods, cold meats and salads of all kinds.

Prawn supplies seemed immune for a time until the arrival of fishing boats from Eastern Europe scoured the bay, estuary and coast clean without a thought for conservation.

LM looked gloomier every time I visited it in the next eight months until independence.

Conditions downtown and most of the middle-class suburbs rapidly deteriorated as services shrank or vanished. Squatters from townships, overcrowded with rural refugees, moved into abandoned city houses and apartments. Rubble and mounting piles of rubbish blocked sidewalks and spilled into streets. The smoke of cooking fires drifted from the upper windows of some downtown apartment blocks.

Mozambique hiccuped along like this under the uneasy partnership of Portugal and Frelimo up to the day of its formal independence, 25 June 1975.

It was another classically African event, all pomp and ceremony amid poverty.

For a week beforehand the city was immersed in a blend of African and Portuguese celebrations. It was bedecked with banners and thousands of copies of the new Frelimo flag, whose centre carried an emblem of a cog (symbolizing industry) surrounding a hoe (agriculture), an open book (learning) and, for the first time on any flag, an AK-47, representing strength.

Delegates streamed in: Dr Alvaro Cunhal, secretary-general of Portugal's communist party and Dr Agostinho Neto, leader of Angola's MPLA, got specially warm welcomes. Others came from places like China, Russia, Bulgaria, Guinea, Yugoslavia, Somalia and the Scandinavian states. Socialists from pink to red dominated.

Some foreign representatives streamed out. The South African consul-general and his staff left in a convoy bound for Ressano Garcia/Komatipoort, leaving only a skeleton staff to handle migrant labour matters and visas.

While all this was going on, Samora Machel was making a month-long whistle-stop tour through Mozambique from north to south talking to jubilant crowds in towns and villages.

■ Top: In their euphoria over imminent independence scores of Mozambicans volunteered to sweep the city streets before the big day.

■ Above centre: A formal guard of honour paraded at the airport to greet important guests arriving for the celebrations.

■ Above: The non-racialism extended to children, like these youngsters taking part in the parades.

■ The carnation, like the one this woman is holding, became the symbol of the Portuguese revolution and freedom of its colonies after troops carried them in the barrels of their guns during the Lisbon coup on 25 April 1974.

WATERSHED

■ Top left: Race was never as divisive a factor in Mozambique as it was in adjacent South Africa and many Mozambicans believed it had a safe multiracial future, such as these two middle-aged ladies among the crowds that gathered on independence day, 25 June.

■ Above: Whites backing Frelimo were in the minority but made their presence known on independence day, this one sporting the flag with an AK-47 on it.

■ Left: Huge banners with Machel's picture and extolling the victory and virtues of Frelimo flowered all over the city where the crowds gathered to watch the celebrations.

■ Right: This Frelimo supporter shows off a copy of *Noticias* with Machel on the front page.

WATERSHED

■ A huge crowd packed the Machava stadium the evening before independence to hear endless rhetoric, fire off guns and the occasional rocket into the air, and for many, to get drunk.

Machel arrived to a huge welcome at the airport the day before the handover. He was especially overjoyed when he was welcomed by smiling Chinese delegates.

This was the day when the word 'mister' disappeared from the local vocabulary, replaced by '*camarada*'.

Machel made his first speech giving pointers to his policy: economic co-operation and neutral co-existence with South Africa. He would oppose apartheid but not assist guerrilla attacks on South Africa.

He was far more militant about Rhodesia: "The struggle of Zimbabwe is our struggle."

That evening saw the biggest public celebration of Mozambique's coming of age, a mass gathering at the Machava stadium to mark the lowering of the Portuguese flag at midnight and the raising of the Frelimo flag. The stadium was lit up like a Christmas tree and filled with a continuous roar of voices and racketing bands.

As the evening progressed the party grew wilder. Some people with AK-47s fired bursts into the air, Palestine style. Ricochetting bullets whizzed around the stadium walls, wounding at least one person.

I was walking outside the main gate when I heard a sizzling roar approach from somewhere inside the stadium. It was a rocket-propelled grenade fired by an enthusiastic fool. It burst in a ball of dirty smoke about ten metres above ground. No one was hurt.

The next day was a standard independence ceremony. Banners festooning the city carried heroic slogans: Down With Elitism, Down With Racism and Imperialism, Viva All Socialist States. In the main plaza the Portuguese and Mozambican flags fluttered behind a dais. A military band led smartly uniformed troops in a march past. Crowds filled the streets and sidewalks around the plaza. Hundreds of people climbed into the spreading branches of the trees at one side.

■ Left: The commander of the Frelimo troops barks his orders on parade in the city's central square where the main celebrations were held.

Machel appeared on the balcony of the city hall, a small figure dwarfed by the tall Grecian pillars on either side and a gigantic picture of himself on the wall behind. He delivered the now standard rhetoric, at great length: "The victory in Mozambique is a victory of the exemplary internationalism of the socialist countries ..." etc, etc.

When he finally finished several 25-pounder howitzers – Second World War guns apparently borrowed from South Africa – fired a smoky 21-gun salute. At the first big bang people fell out of the nearby trees like ripe fruit.

The Portuguese flag dropped slowly and the Mozambican flag rose in its place. Mozambique was independent – a basket case but 'free'.

The freedom was largely symbolic and the day's huff and puff was hot air. For all the verbal bluster the socialist state could do very little. They had to depend heavily on South Africa.

The final irony was that South Africa was also covertly supporting a new challenge to Frelimo: Renamo, the Mozambique National Resistance Movement initiated by the Rhodesians. That little internal war went on for 15 years – Pretoria was having it both ways.

> The Portuguese flag dropped slowly, the Mozambique flag rising in its place. Mozambique was independent – a basket case but 'free'.

■ Frelimo soldiers on parade.

■ Facing: After the formal signing Joaquim Chissano, a suave and elegant speaker, addresses a press conference where he outlines Frelimo's policy of neutral co-existence with South Africa but support for the anti-Rhodesian forces.

■ Left: Deputy President Joaquim Chissano formally takes over the country from Portugal at a ceremony in the governor's residence. Vice Admiral Victor Crespo, Portugal's retiring governor, is behind him.

■ Above: Part of Frelimo's women's brigade in an unusual marching formation with hands clasped. The banners are about establishing people's power to serve the masses and unity plus organization forming an impenetrable wall.

■ Left: Bandsmen take a break between bouts of martial music.

■ One of the cheerleaders was this bespectacled, academic-looking MPLA soldier with his finger incautiously on the trigger of his RPG launcher.

PART III
ANGOLA

The coup in Lisbon hit Angola with the force of a sucker punch to the solar plexus. It left the country breathless, shocked and in disarray.

Blacks were delighted: colonialism had been a bitter existence for them as the main source of slaves for Brazil and then cheap labour. Whites were alarmed, especially the many who made their wealth from government patronization. The sizeable population of *mestiços* or *mulattos*, people of mixed blood of whom many were assimilated with white culture, were confused, unable to fathom where their future lay.

For weeks no one knew what was happening bar the fact that the generals had taken over in Portugal and were forming a junta. Life, however, briefly carried on as usual before it began to hiccup and stumble like a car running out of fuel.

Angola was not a largely backward country like Mozambique, neglected for centuries and now living on the thin economic cream of service to its neighbours. It was better developed than any other African state except South Africa, Rhodesia and possibly Namibia. It could stand on its own economically. It might have been politically viable too if the differences between its warring factions could be resolved – improbable but not impossible.

The conflict in the country between Portugal and the three main liberation movements had ground almost to stasis, not quite a stalemate, rather a marking of time when none of the four was either progressing or retreating. Each of the liberation movements held fluctuating sway over pieces of territory but none firmly enough to claim control. The Portuguese forces could go anywhere they wanted, if they wanted, which often they did not because it could be arduous and dangerous. They were suffering from extended lines, limited manpower, massive expense and ennui.

So daily routine continued until it began to crumble when the indecision, confusion and incompetence reigning in Lisbon spread to Africa. My colleagues and I watched Angola's administration start to fall rapidly apart in a matter of months as civil servants in rural areas received contradictory orders or none at all. Many tried to carry on as usual but it was without direction.

Most did nothing. Many quit.

The Lisbon junta had appointed a co-ordinating committee – a local junta – to run Angola and sent out Admiral Rosa Coutinho as its high commissioner. He soon became known as 'Rosa the Red' or 'The Red Admiral' because of his blatant favouring of the left-wing MPLA.

■ Admiral 'Rosa the Red' Coutinho, Portugal's first high commissioner to Angola after the Lisbon coup.

Its authority outside Luanda, however, was tenuous at best, except where Portugal still had garrisons. And even there its control was dubious because many of their troops, restive at being kept on when their war was over, were beginning to take sides. Most had stopped shooting and were staying put in their barracks, bases, camps and little fortresses scattered all over the country. What was the point in fighting?

In their various areas of influence, the MPLA, FNLA and UNITA guerrillas began coming out into the open. In eastern and southern Angola Dr Jonas Savimbi met visitors entering from Zambia who were able to see for themselves some of the results of UNITA attacks.

■ Right: Guerrillas cross the wreckage of a road bridge.

■ Below: Somewhere in eastern Angola, near the Zaire and Zambian borders, UNITA men examine a road bridge they had blasted earlier in the war. The scene is reminiscent of a famous poster of a collapsed railway bridge.

■ Top: Dr Jonas Savimbi, UNITA leader, left, and his men examine a pair of their 75mm recoilless rifles. Easy to use and highly portable, they were very effective.

■ Above: The Portuguese erected statues in just about every centre in Angola, like this one of some unidentified public figure which UNITA toppled when they took over the central town of Nova Lisboa.

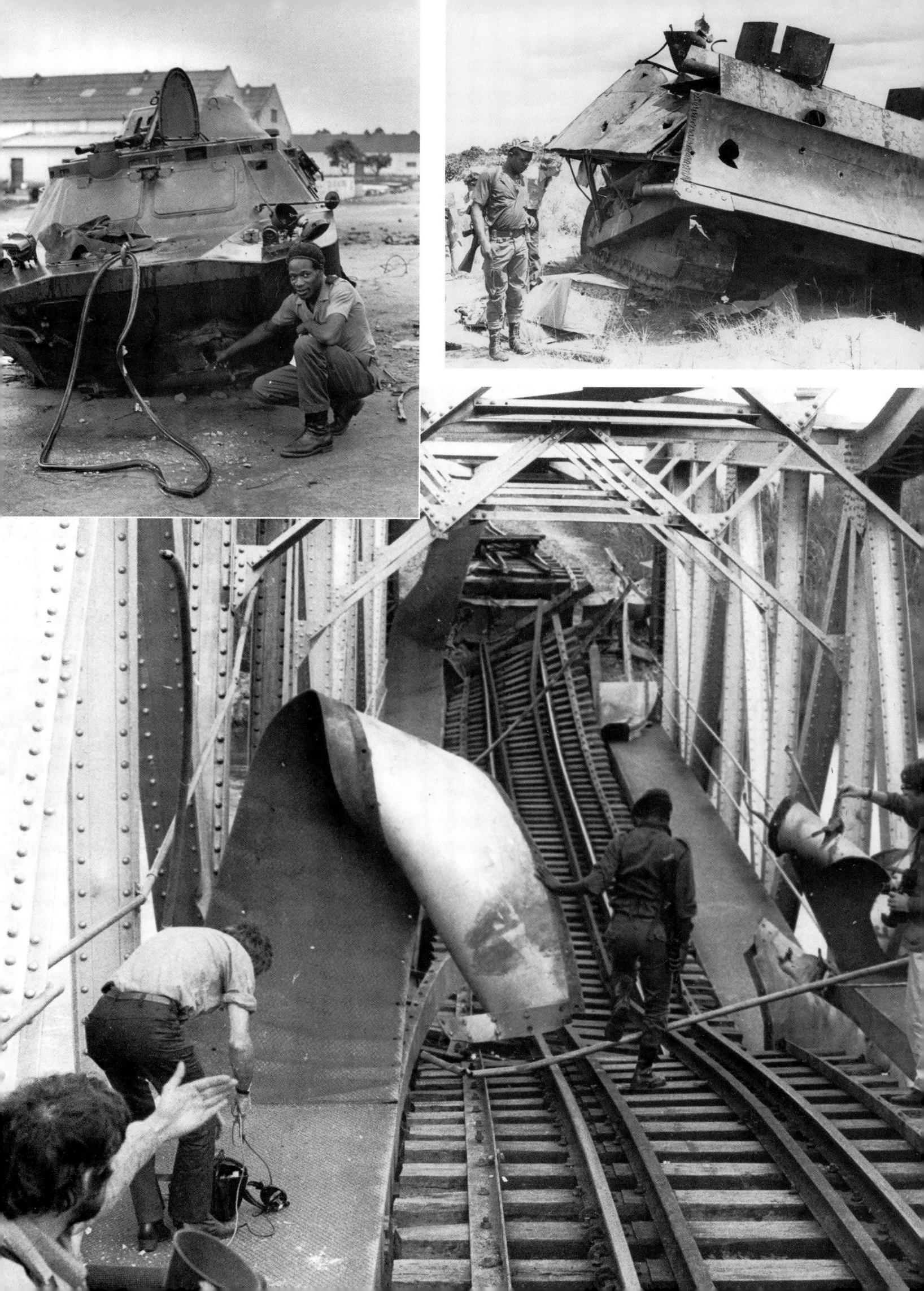

■ **Far left:** A UNITA guerrilla shows where a shell penetrated an MPLA armoured vehicle knocked out by UNITA in Nova Lisboa when they seized the city.

■ **Left:** Guerrillas of all three liberation movements made Heath Robinson use of anything they could to bolster their armaments. The bulldozer was converted into a crude tank by the MPLA but had no chance of survival against modern weapons.

■ **Below:** UNITA shows off what it can do. This thoroughly demolished bridge is on the Benguela railroad somewhere in eastern Angola near Zaire and Zambia.

Pressure built fast in the first several months as the three rebel movements hastened to consolidate their authority in their respective operational areas and clashed when they met. The FNLA busied themselves in the north and northeast, especially among the million-strong Bakongo tribe, half of whom were in Zaire. In the southern third of the country, home of the Ovimbundu group of tribes, Savimbi effectively asserted his personality and his UNITA movement and extended his activity to the east.

The MPLA did not bind itself to any ethnic group. Under Dr Agostinho Neto's canny guidance they focused on urban areas – particularly among the hungry and frustrated folk of the teeming slums, the blue-collars and the intelligentsia – as well as in some rural areas in the east and along the coast. Ultimately it proved to be the winning formula, backed by a massive supply of Soviet weapons, but only after much bloodshed.

By October 1974 all had established loosely defined regions but it became clear that national power could not be achieved without control of the capital, Luanda, where the MPLA already had a foothold.

Any option other than the big three evaporated rapidly. The last twitches were by a group calling themselves the Christian Democrats and by the Front for the Liberation of Cabinda (FLEC), the small, densely forested Angolan enclave just north of the Congo River.

The Christian Democrats, a small, hard-core right-wing group were perhaps the dumbest political party in Angola's history. They planned to use weapons smuggled ashore in fishing boats to capture an arms' store in the city with the help of ex-members of the DGS secret police and then take over the city.

They began by witlessly placing an advertisement in the country's biggest newspaper asking people to join them and supply details of their military background and training.

Naturally they were arrested. Their plot would not have worked anyway. The arms shipment never materialized and the arms' store in the city held only 230 weapons.

The FLEC made their last-ditch bid for Cabinda's independence late in October. They mounted a mass protest in the town of Cabinda against the arrival of three MPLA officials to open an office there. The local governor, Brigadier Themudo Barata, sent troops to quell the demonstration.

Junior Portuguese officers, agitated by rumour and misinformation about the FLEC's intentions, sided with the MPLA, sacked their own commanders and marched their troops on Cabinda town, supported by a company of well-armed MPLA guerrillas. They arrested Brigadier Barata and his officers, took control of the radio station, post office, police station, airport and access roads and virtually installed the MPLA as the rulers in Cabinda.

The incident severely embarrassed the Angolan and Lisbon juntas because it made the supposedly impartial military appear to back the MPLA. Serious bloodshed looked imminent and the last thing Lisbon wanted was its olive branch shot off.

But the incident was pushed to the back burner in the next few days when the big three began their moves into Luanda, turning its airport into a political circus and the city into a killing ground.

In Luanda the junta's powers were feeble. *Muçeques* – the slum townships surrounding the landward sides of the city – devolved into no-go zones where tribal and political fighting and raging crime dominated. An estimated half a million people lived there, with more refugees from the rural areas flooding in daily. What little policing existed was replaced by murder, robbery and rape. Troops attempted to impose some semblance of order but could enter only in armed vehicle patrols by day. By night mayhem ruled.

The FNLA was the first to flex its muscle in the city. An advance party headed by Hendrik Vaal Neto landed at Luanda airport in early November to be met by a roaring crowd estimated to number about 4,000, but which I guessed was at least 6,000, who filled the terminal and its surrounds.

On 4 November – 13 years after Holden Roberto's guerrillas bloodily massacred hundreds of people in northern Angola – they opened an office, ratcheting up the tension.

They did it with arrogance, slapping down the gauntlet to the other movements. About 4,000 supporters paraded their leaders through the city streets into one of the most violence-ridden *muçeques*, sweeping up more people as they went.

Prancing and dancing, causing massive traffic tangles, they marched to the Avenida do Brazil, the scene of much criminal activity in recent months, where they occupied most of the third floor of an office block.

They picked the place deliberately. Metres past its entrance 'safe' Luanda ended. Beyond that the broad avenue stretched on into the *muçeque* and to certain death for any outsider foolish enough to wander there.

I stood on that invisible line several times and looked down the avenue through a telephoto lens. Young blacks, some small children, saw me and immediately began performing, dancing from foot to foot, waving sticks and machetes. Definitely no place to go.

The tension in Luanda soared when the news broke that an MPLA team, including some of its leading members, would arrive a few days later, on 8 November, to open their headquarters in the city.

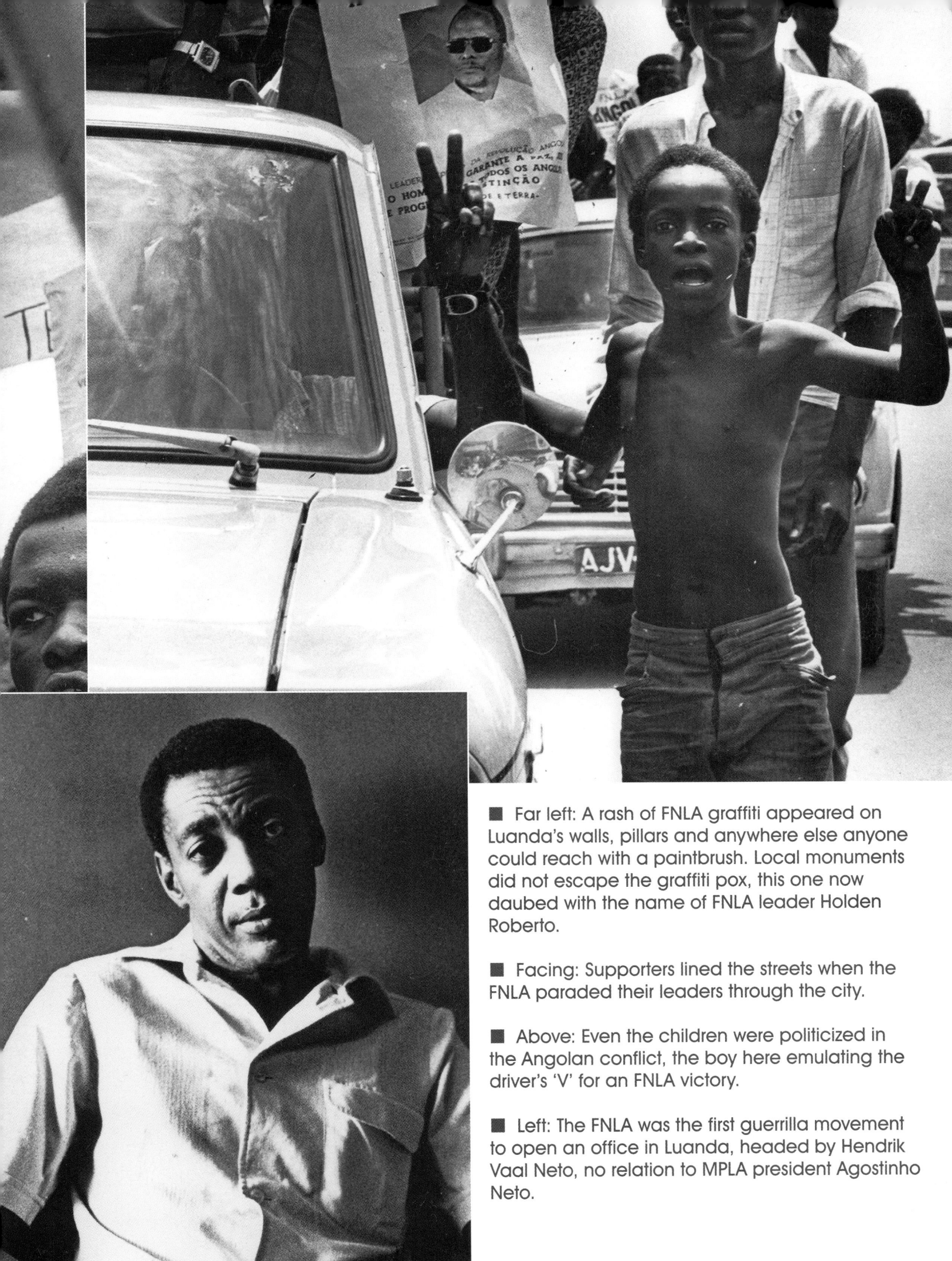

■ Far left: A rash of FNLA graffiti appeared on Luanda's walls, pillars and anywhere else anyone could reach with a paintbrush. Local monuments did not escape the graffiti pox, this one now daubed with the name of FNLA leader Holden Roberto.

■ Facing: Supporters lined the streets when the FNLA paraded their leaders through the city.

■ Above: Even the children were politicized in the Angolan conflict, the boy here emulating the driver's 'V' for an FNLA victory.

■ Left: The FNLA was the first guerrilla movement to open an office in Luanda, headed by Hendrik Vaal Neto, no relation to MPLA president Agostinho Neto.

The Lisbon and local juntas had, for several months, been frantically attempting to cobble together a transitional government comprising the three movements and, to avoid whites fleeing en masse, representatives of the country's half million whites.

The effort was stillborn. They had to negotiate separately with each of the the three movements because they refused to meet together. Talks deadlocked from the start over how many representatives each would have and who would be the interim prime minister and eventually the president.

While this was going on the few remaining seams of order in the city were bulging dangerously. Word began to trickle in of violence elsewhere in Angola.

At the Duke of Braganza village east of Luanda whites abandoned their farms and holed up in two tourist hotels after mob violence killed at least six people. Armed gangs roamed the region. There and at Cela to the south blacks demanded that whites leave immediately. Similar incidents were taking place elsewhere.

By now it was obvious to all except the most obsessive optimists that Angola was plunging toward civil war. All three movements wanted total and exclusive power. Under heavy pressure from the international community, especially Portugal and African nations like Kenya and Zambia, they were going through the motions of negotiation but without commitment. They went to meetings in Kinshasa, Nairobi and Lusaka and issued statements favouring a transitional government. It was a charade.

The rising pressures in Luanda sent ripples far and wide. Suddenly it was major front-page news under swelling headlines.

On 8 November the MPLA delegation arrived in a blaze of hysteria to formally open their Luanda headquarters. The crowd at Luanda's Belas airport to meet the chartered Zambian Airways plane from Brazzaville was like the crowd at an FA Cup final. By the time the plane landed three hours late a frenzied mass of people jammed every available space. The army estimated it at about 30,000. I thought it could be double that. There was no way of making an accurate count.

A dense carpet of humanity swarmed over and around the terminal buildings like bees on honey. They packed on the roofs. They clambered up the tall floodlight standards to cling like fruit to the batteries of the lamps on top. They spilled over on to the airport apron. They waved thousands

■ Top: A young FNLA guerrilla guards the entrance to the building where the FNLA has set up its Luanda headquarters.

■ Left: There is no way of knowing whether the man in his cups is shouting for or against the FNLA.

of paper MPLA flags. Their cheering rose in a continuous roar. Their enthusiasm was undampened by the thick, muggy heat.

Scheduled flights landing en route to Europe had to be delayed or diverted.

Fearing trouble, Portuguese troops had appeared in force on central Luanda's streets the previous day and patrolled the fringes of the *muçeques*. On the day itself security at the airport was tight: a barrier of troops blocked entry to the terminal, trying unsuccessfully to deny people through without an official pass and a body search. Nearby, out of sight of the crowd, armed soldiers stood ready in case of trouble.

Tom Roy and I found ourselves jammed with other foreign correspondents inside a mass of yelling, sweating, gesticulating people, at times so tightly we could barely move our arms. Luckily they were in a bouyant mood, full of happy grins.

After a brief welcome inside the terminal, where the air was like a sauna bath, the delegates were whisked off with a strong escort to a modest house in the notorious Rangel *muçeque*, their new headquarters.

■ When the plane arrived the huge crowd poured on to the airfield as it taxied to a stop, simply shoving aside a cordon of 3,000 Portuguese soldiers around the apron before the engines had been turned off.

■ Risking death by electrocution or plunge, hundreds of MPLA supporters climbed into the clusters of floodlights around the terminal to get a good view of the Zambian Airways plane landing, while Portuguese officers monitored the situation from an Alouette III helicopter.

■ Above: A giant poster of MPLA president Dr Agostinho Neto adorned the front of the crammed Belas airport terminal at Luanda before the Zambian Airways bringing the MPLA delegation plane touched down.

■ Above right: To add to the festive atmosphere at the Belas terminal local pop bands provided a non-stop programme of music.

■ Right: Support for the MPLA crossed racial boundaries, as this woman shows, though not many whites followed it.

■ If there was any doubt before about the MPLA's overwhelming popularity in Luanda, it was thoroughly dispelled by the enormous welcome their delegates received at the airport and in the city. Here MPLA guerrillas exhort the excited crowd to new fervour while waiting for their representatives to emerge from the terminal.

Two days later, a Sunday, UNITA's delegates arrived at the airport led by the 23-year-old Dr Fernando Wilson. The Luanda boiler blew.

Their arrival was smaller than the MPLA's but considerably larger than the FNLA's. Crowds streamed to the airport, nearly half of them whites, and by the time UNITA's team arrived at noon they numbered close to twenty thousand.

There would have been more had the MPLA not racked up the tension another few notches by deliberately challenging UNITA. They had been celebrating noisily without pause for two days after their own delegates' arrival and from early on the Sunday morning UNITA supporters responded, roaring through city streets in cars and trucks with hooters blaring, waving big pictures of Savimbi and the UNITA flag of red and green with a black cockerel and sunrise centrepiece.

Tempers flared near the airport just before UNITA's plane touched down. A group of locals found a white man carrying a gun, surrounded him and stripped him naked. Military police rushed to his rescue firing shots in the air to disperse them. Hundreds of blacks ran in panic.

Some were injured. Ambulances and truckloads of troops arrived and MPLA supporters held an impromptu meeting beside the airport road, hastening the exodus.

The UNITA delegates rode to their office in the city centre in a noisy procession that caused a monumental traffic jam for hours. Cavalcades of trucks heaped top-heavy with yelling, flag-waving people travelled the main streets, scattering pro-Savimbi leaflets. The deafening blast of hooters went on late into the night.

The new UNITA office was close to the Tivoli Hotel and, somewhat to our dismay, right above our office.

■ When we arrived one morning at the entrance to the building where we had an office we found these two smartly-clad young UNITA men with large 9mm pistols guarding it. They were very friendly and promised to look after us too. We wondered whether their presence would give protection or bring trouble.

■ A woman makes no bones about where her support lies.

■ UNITA graffiti appeared in Luanda wherever the FNLA and MPLA had not beaten them to it and here includes the names of leader Jonas Malheiro Savimbi and his deputy, Nzau Puna.

All that weekend violence simmered. The night before the UNITA team's arrival cars had been stoned in and around the *muçeques*, an old man was badly beaten and a top hockey player and a truck driver were burned to death in their vehicles.

During the night after UNITA's arrival the city's remaining seams of law and order split apart. Armed gangs, fuelled by the political hype, raged through the *muçeques* hunting down their opponents. Portuguese troops were ordered to patrol them and other suburbs with instructions to "punish" troublemakers. In the notorious Avenida do Brazil jeep-loads of FNLA guerrillas arrived uninvited to help them, using the opportunity to take pot shots at MPLA supporters.

At least 48 people were killed that night – 27 by bullets and the rest more gruesomely by clubs, machetes and fire. The unofficial figure was up to fifty-seven. Later one military spokesman said more than a hundred had been killed and several times that number wounded, while another spokesman stuck to the figure of forty-eight. There was no hope of an accurate count; the Portuguese authorities had never kept detailed records of their slum populace or even taken a cursory census. People vanished there without trace.

My staffers saw a makeshift mortuary in the city, a room stuffed almost ceiling-high with corpses.

Keeping accurate track of the violence was close to impossible. It was tricky and we trod warily. At times we almost walked into shoot-outs with bullets ricochetting off buildings. Usually we were forewarned by bursts of automatic gunfire.

Life was cheap and the prospect of recovery from injury, with the kind of medical care available, was chilling. There were ample examples of what happened to the incautious.

The city was a powder keg. Murder and mayhem continued. Troops rushing to a house where a child had been killed by blacks were met by a burst of automatic rifle fire; they returned fired, killing two men. Gangs from the slums petrol bombed more than six homes in the middle-class Catambor suburb in retaliation for the killing of a black man. Angry residents berated troops guarding firemen fighting the fires.

A day later all 200 families in Catambor abandoned their homes, which slum dwellers promptly looted. Next day the residents of another suburb, white and mulatto, fled because they also bordered a *muçeque*.

After at least one soldier was killed and seven wounded in the *muçeques* an 18h00 curfew was imposed, making travel risky. Soldiers shot at cars breaking it.

Compounding the general chaos and confusion, up in Cabinda former FLEC guerrillas attacked a garrison,

killing two men and captured key gun emplacements. They took 39 hostages and repeated the FLEC's demand for an independent Cabinda.

Admiral Coutinho and his junta loftily watched all this from their eyrie in the oldest part of Luanda, the fortress of St Miguel. He and his junta decided that there was no point in trying to create a transitional government and suspended negotiations.

The military briefings there became less and less informative as control over Angola slipped steadily from the junta's hands.

Two days later Luanda calmed a little as the three liberation movements took a breather, assessed the situation and brought in reinforcements. Violence continued at a lower level.

UNITA brought in more than six busloads of men in civilian clothes "to help keep the suburbs quiet". Translated, this meant they would shoot anyone who opposed them.

The FNLA brought about 200 men from Zaire in a passenger jet which departed with 300 local recruits leaving for training.

Only the MPLA did not fetch reinforcements. They didn't need to, they had ample informal fighters in the *muçeques*.

Mid-week tensions rose again as Luandans faced the prospect of another eruption at the weekend, the time most *muçeque* dwellers seemed to favour for making trouble.

In the *muçeques* life was a hellish saga of survival against enemies and hunger. Most of the small trading

stores run by Portuguese and mulattos had been shut, looted or burned, or all three. Many of the communal taps were dry. Streets were blocked by rubble and wrecked cars. Nights were punctuated by gunfire.

There were rumours that at least one of the liberation movements had been recruiting mercenaries, raising the grim prospect of another Katanga-like conflict. The army discounted this but warned the three that civil war loomed.

■ Above: Perched atop a bluff overlooking the Atlantic, the fortress of St Miguel was the Portuguese military headquarters in Angola. A lovely, irregular, white-painted structure of thick, sloped walls and five arrowhead bastions, it was over four centuries old. Inside were cool white courtyards and spacious rooms with antique blue-and-white wall tiles depicting historic scenes. It was staffed by officers in spick-and-span uniforms. Bloodshed might have been a world away.

■ Right: This confident fellow sporting a chic cigarette holder carries an old but still efficient Russian PPSh-41 sub-machine gun.

WATERSHED

■ Above: His uniform and cap are Portuguese but the gumboots and AK-47 are a giveaway: he's a guerrilla, but for whom?

■ Above right: Proud of the AK-47s issued to them, used but still good, new MPLA recruits in Luanda show off for the photographer.

■ Right: Guerrillas did not hesitate to search anyone on the street they thought might be carrying a weapon.

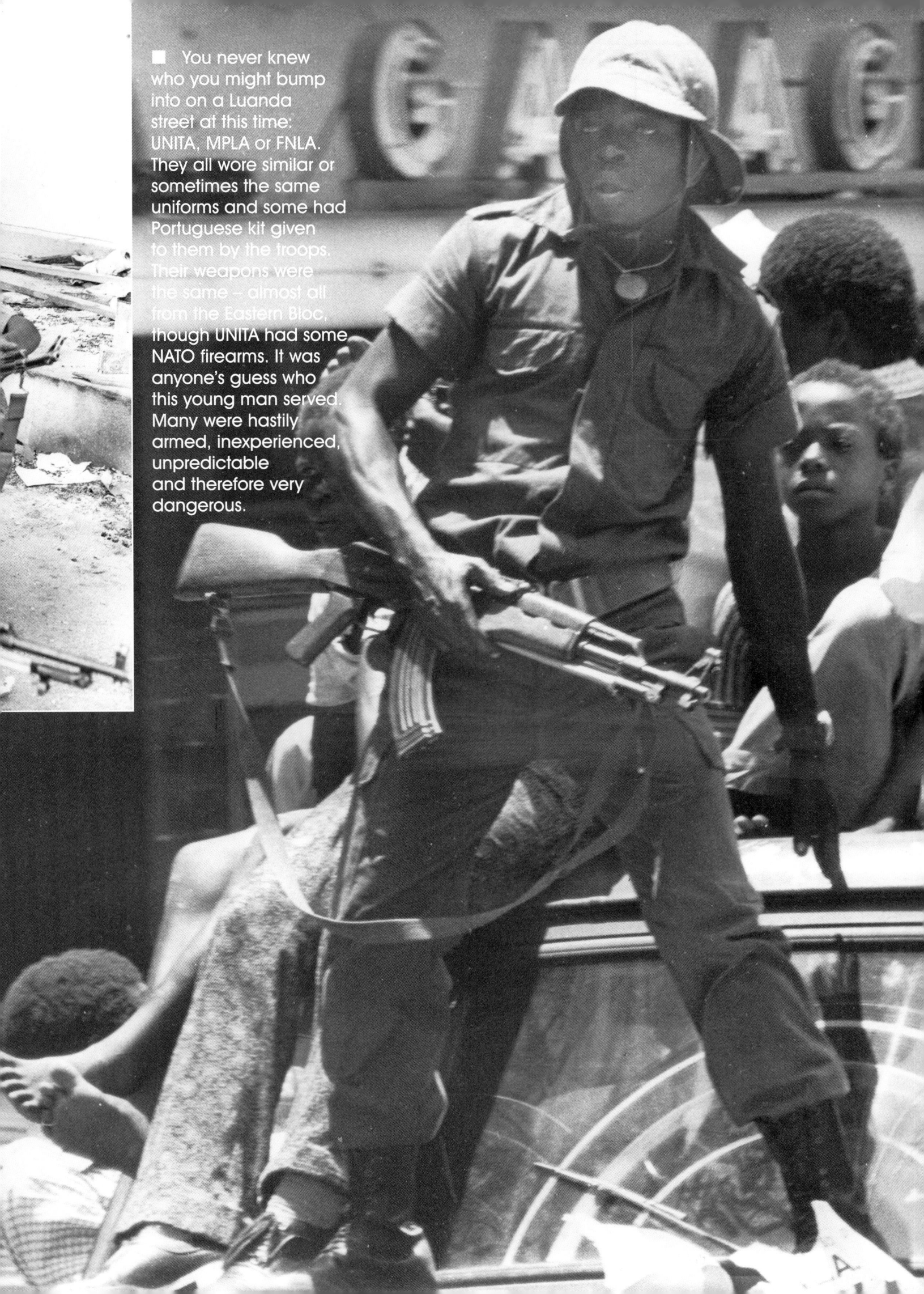

■ You never knew who you might bump into on a Luanda street at this time: UNITA, MPLA or FNLA. They all wore similar or sometimes the same uniforms and some had Portuguese kit given to them by the troops. Their weapons were the same — almost all from the Eastern Bloc, though UNITA had some NATO firearms. It was anyone's guess who this young man served. Many were hastily armed, inexperienced, unpredictable and therefore very dangerous.

The MPLA asserted its growing authority in Luanda by setting up roadblocks on routes to the city. Here they check reporter José Ricardo, amiably but firm and not to be challenged.

The danger of civil war was echoed by Portugal's new Minister for Overseas Territories, Dr Almeida Santos: "If it is not possible to maintain a balance between the three in the political field, I can see only one alternative which we want to avoid at all costs – civil war."

Many Portuguese had already packed up and gone. The wealthier suburbs were shrinking as residents left with all the moveable possessions they could ship out and locked their doors behind them with no hope of selling their homes.

Those remaining made a show of going about their business and the city-centre shops and sidewalk cafés were busy. There was only one subject of discussion over the coffee cups: how to escape the collapsing world around them. Life continued but with nervous overtones and growing shortages of simple consumer goods like orange juice, beer, matches and vegetables.

Many black employees failed to turn up for work and had left town. Flights to Lisbon were booked solid for the next six weeks. The black market rate for the Angolan *escudo* rose sharply.

So jittery were Luanda whites that when two Africans entered a Portuguese carpenter's shop and asked to see the owner, the owner excused himself, fetched a shotgun and shot both men dead.

The Portuguese army suddenly flexed its muscle. Strong forces of troops with orders to shoot tried precariously to defuse the racial and political bomb. Armoured cars trundled through the perimeter streets and alleys of the shantytowns watched by sullen locals who had already driven out all the whites there. Some were big eight-wheeled Panhards with 75mm cannon, others armoured troop carriers and the remainder Chaimites and small Panhards.

■ The rifle he carries is a NATO-issue G3, German design, some were made in Portugal under licence, which probably makes the man a UNITA guerrilla.

■ Above: Portuguese troops assemble in a city street prepatory to going on patrol in the suburbs to give some protection to residents where violence was spreading.

■ Below: A Portuguese private holds up a captured AK-47.

■ Left: Proud of their perfectly laced boots, soldiers armed with G3 rifles wait to go on patrol on the back of a Unimog.

■ Top: A soldier breaking into an apparently abandoned apartment in Luanda to check if anyone is inside wants his rifle before he goes any further.

■ Above: Soldiers and guerrillas tried to maintain good relations; they were no longer at war. Here a soldier in an armoured car accepts a cigarette from a guerrilla holding a petrol bomb.

The year 1974 stumbled into 1975 in a rumble of rhetoric and gunfire that verged on open warfare. Only the presence of the Portuguese, determined to stay in Angola until the designated date for independence – 11 November – kept it in some semblance of check for a few months.

Militarily, the three movements were hugely different. The FNLA, the oldest, had an estimated 10–15,000 soldiers trained by Chinese instructors in Zaire. The MPLA had massive support from urban militants and some 5,000 guerrillas. UNITA had strong backing among the tribes of the south and perhaps 1,000 trained guerrillas.

A spokesman for the the junta in Angola, Captain Vasco Gonçalves, denounced the FNLA for bringing armed forces into the city and threatened to stop all the movements from doing so (conveniently ignoring that the MPLA had already armed thousands of civilians). Unsurprisingly, no one paid him the slightest heed and UNITA started building its local strength.

The political wheeling and dealing continued for months without any success because none of the movements wanted unity. The leaders went to meeting after meeting in Kenya, Zaire, Portugal and elsewhere to placate the African states and Lisbon junta, not forgetting the Americans and Russians who were now tentatively sticking their fingers into the pie.

Each said they wanted a single united Angola without any breakaways like Cabinda. Each claimed support across tribal, ideological and racial lines. Each condemned the rash of wildcat strikes erupting across the country, particularly at ports. Each wanted full economic development based on Angola's considerable mineral and agricultural assets. Each 'wanted' peace.

And each wanted all the power unto themselves.

Yet despite this, the Portuguese managed to get the three together in Portugal on 15 January 1975 to sign a precarious unity titled the Alvor Agreement. They pledged to form a transitional government to independence with equal shares in a prime ministerial council, ministries and a national army beefed up by 24,000 Portuguese soldiers. Their job would be to draw up a constitution, register voters and hold elections in October for a constituent assembly.

The print was barely dry when it collapsed.

A month after the signing, MPLA forces loyal to Dr Neto attacked their own bureau in Luanda to drive out members of a splinter group led by Daniel Chipenda, killing fifteen. Chipenda promptly joined the FNLA as an assistant secretary-general and took his rabble to southeast Angola near the Zambian border.

Early in 1975 Roberto's FNLA launched a tirade of propaganda against the MPLA, buying a Luanda newspaper and TV station with American money, thereby placing the US in the strange position of backing the same horse as China, which had supplied the FNLA with tons of arms. The FNLA proclaimed itself the keeper of law and order and ferociously condemned the MPLA. Simultaneously, it moved thousands of troops from Zaire into towns and villages in northern and central Angola, including a motorized column of 500 men into Luanda itself.

This bellicosity could have only one result. It began with clashes between FNLA and MPLA troops in two Luanda *muçeques* from March 1975. Soon after this about 50 MPLA men were massacred in a village to the north.

The slum warfare erupted throughout the Luanda *muçeques* when the FNLA attacked all the MPLA's offices. It continued into May with intermittent ceasefires between concerted attacks that left about 700 dead and 1,000 wounded.

The FNLA onslaught was not confined to Luanda. They fell upon the MPLA in towns and villages in the north, at Nova Lisboa in the centre and as far south and east as the towns along the Benguela railway eastward to Teixeira de Sousa. For good measure they also attacked UNITA forces in the far south at Lobito.

Portugal again summoned the party leaders to persuade them to resume the Alvor Agreement. UNITA's Savimbi – understandably, as his was the weakest army – became the strongest advocate of peaceful settlement. He met Neto and Roberto at Nakuru in Kenya in June where they signed yet another agreement to create a 'climate of peace'.

Two days later the shooting resumed more viciously than before. The MPLA counter-attacked and gun battles raged in Luanda's *muçeques*, in the FNLA stronghold of Carmona, in a number of other centres and in the Cabinda enclave where the MPLA had been in control for some time.

In June UNITA was dragged firmly into the fray when the MPLA struck at their Luanda office (right above ours), killing some of their men.

The MPLA had been smuggling Soviet-supplied weapons wholesale into Angola for months. Hundreds of tons were shipped or flown into the former French Congo, Congo-Brazzaville, then smuggled south into Angola by plane and road. More than six Eastern Bloc ships landed arms for the MPLA virtually under the noses of the Portuguese whose will and military strength were by now so sapped they could not or would not do anything to stop the trafficking. There was suspicion that the Portuguese

■ Top left: Looters flee from the Portuguese forces chasing them out of suburban areas. It was a hopeless task: they returned as soon as the soldiers' backs were turned.

■ Above: A tearful woman looks at the wreckage of her home in a Luanda suburb after it was looted by rioters from the *muçeques*. A soldier and a neighbour try to console her but she has lost everything of value.

■ The impact of urban warfare: Shell Oil storage tanks just outside Luanda near the harbour burn after taking gunfire during a clash between MPLA and FNLA guerrillas.

were resigned to accepting MPLA dominance – certainly some backed the MPLA.

It was very well organized. The weapons went to destinations in so many parts of Angola that the MPLA was able to launch a widespread onslaught from late July through August, which drove the FNLA out of Luanda and pushed them back in the north. Simultaneously, it evicted UNITA from all major towns and ports along the southern Angolan coast, also casting inland and taking virtual control of central Angola. It already had Cabinda firmly under its thumb.

■ Above: Some houses in suburbs near the *muçeques* took heavy crossfire during the fighting between the guerrilla movements. This balcony (left) was struck by automatic rifle fire and grenades and the damage to a popular restaurant and café is examined by a Portuguese soldier (right).

■ Left: Many Luandans lost their vehicles, and sometimes their lives in the gun battles between the MPLA and FNLA. Cars were riddled with bullets, hit by rockets or grenades and overturned and burned.

Drained by political in-fighting at home, struggling to contain an unsympathetic public, Lisbon could do nothing to stop the avalanche of conflict. The ruling junta gave up trying to make peace between the patently incompatible movements and let matters take their own course. In August Admiral Leonel Cardoso was sent to Luanda as high commissioner, a rubber-stamp spectator.

Come hell or high water Angola would get its independence on 11 November 1975, at which time all Portuguese troops would be withdrawn, Lisbon decreed. Admiral Cardoso and his entourage would be the last to leave, aboard a warship.

A round, genial little man, the admiral was very approachable but told us little of importance.

By the end of September, the three movements had settled into uneasy dominance over loosely defined chunks of the country. The MPLA ruled in Luanda and about a dozen district capitals, including the other key ports of Lobito and Moçamedes.

The FNLA held sway in large rural areas north and northeast of the capital up to the Congo River and the Congo-Kinshasa border and was skirmishing with the MPLA for control of places like Carmona, centre of the coffee-growing region.

Fattened with more weapons ferried to it through Zaire by America, the FNLA was still a force to be reckoned with. It had the largest number of men under arms, though their training and discipline were poor and they had a mix of weaponry from different sources. Despite this, their guerrillas pushed to about 25 kilometres north of Luanda near a small place named Quifandongo, the main source of Luanda's water supply.

The MPLA had forced UNITA out of all the towns and villages it occupied except for several along the Benguela railway, where fighting was

■ South African troops guarding the Kunene River hydro-electric scheme created jointly by the South African and Portuguese governments before the Lisbon coup d'etat. It is upstream of the point where the river becomes the border between Angola and Namibia at the Ruacana Falls and continues from there to the Atlantic.

WATERSHED

continuing. UNITA had effectively been driven back into its original role as a bush-based guerrilla movement in the south and east.

This, then, was the situation by late September: the MPLA dominating urban areas, giving it the most political clout; the FNLA largely bottled up in the north and northeast with its big but inefficient army; the small though competent UNITA guerrilla force locked into the southern Ovimbundu tribal area of mostly bush and swamp.

They clashed along the fringes of their respective areas. Small towns and villages changed hands like chips in a poker game and this near stalemate could have gone on indefinitely, a fairly standard African political mess.

What changed it was the decision by world powers to stick their noses in, which immediately elevated Angola to the status of a Cold War battlefield. China sensibly stayed out and withdrew its instructors who had been training FNLA soldiers in Zaire. Arms began streaming to both the FNLA and UNITA from the USA and to the MPLA from the Soviet Union. Some black states also contributed weapons to the parties of their choice.

Washington was in a dilemma. It had no wish to become directly involved in a grubby little African conflict. Americans were still licking their psychological wounds after the Vietnam débâcle and would react angrily if their involvement became public knowledge. But nor did it want to leave a clear field to the Soviets.

So the Gerald Ford government entered into an unholy secret agreement with Pretoria for South African forces to go in to stem to Red tide.

It was, in the clarity of retrospect, a disastrous decision. Africa was relatively unimportant beside the main issues at stake in the Cold War and the stakes involved in Africa were too small to warrant heavy commitment by either side. The effect of this action was to escalate the conflict from a relatively low-key confrontation into an intense, almost conventional war that became an international issue, lasted for decades and almost devastated Angola.

Washington's covert approval played right into the hands of the rising power within the South African government and its defence minister P. W. Botha. This arrogant and bellicose man had steadily spent billions to build up the South African Defence Force (SADF) into the most efficient and best equipped in all Africa.

He had a huge military machine and generals straining at the leash but nothing to launch it against, nothing to conquer. Botha was limited to minor assistance to the UDI regime in Rhodesia in their war against black guerrillas and to policing the South West African border with Angola and Zambia – a tricky task because of that territory's internationally disputed status.

South African forces had been crossing into southern Angola in hot pursuit of SWAPO guerrillas for some time. In August 1975 Botha sent troops to guard the Ruacana Falls hydro-electric plant, a joint project between South Africa and the now defunct Portugese dictatorship on the Kunene River a few kilometres inside Angola.

God knows how many people died in these months, which were to be the birthing of the civil war that reduced this country of such great potential to rubble. It might have been thousands given the intensity of the fighting in which not only rifles but also mortars, rocket-propelled grenades and light artillery were used. The Alvor Agreement, the transitional government and the country were in shreds with refugees from the battles streaming in all directions.

Ken Feil, a large *Washington Post* photographer on loan to me, was invited to the southeast by Daniel Chipenda, the leader of the group who broke off from the MPLA. Chipenda was in Luanda allegedly for peace talks and was impressed by Ken's array of *Washington Post* dogtags.

Ken flew off south with him. For days I heard nothing. A man could simply vanish into eternity down there.

A week later Ken sauntered in with the only photos of that group. They appeared to do little or nothing but sit around.

■ Above left: Chipenda's men seemed happy enough to do little and enjoy their meals.

■ Above: MPLA splinter group leader Daniel Chipenda, who linked up with the FNLA, explains his philosophies at a camp in the bush somewhere in the far southeast of Angola.

■ Left: Chipenda's men wander on patrol past a farmhouse destroyed in earlier fighting.

Portuguese were leaving in a rising stream, packing their possessions in crates and shipping them out or selling what they could. Many took what wealth they were able to translate into illegal diamonds or into airline tickets still being sold, strangely, at the official exchange rate.

And yet central Luanda remained a weird island of false calm. Some of the fighting raging in the *muçeques* spilled over its edges but the remaining white residents continued their farce of normality: shopping, cruising the dwindling number of cafés still open and partying as if they were not surrounded by bloodshed.

■ Above: Killed in the 1974 fighting, this skeleton lay for months on the steps of the old fortress of Sao Pedro do Barra from where slaves used to be loaded on board ships for transport to Brazil. Most slaves were captured inland by tribes such as the Bakongo and sold to the Portuguese. The skeleton was probably of a woman.

■ Left: In late 1975 I was driving around the outskirts of Luanda near the burning oil tanks with Reg Shay, a freelance foreign correspondent, when we saw this remnant of a victim of the earlier fighting near the ancient coastal slave trading fortress of Sao Pedro do Barra. It had been picked clean by scavengers except for a patch of hair on top. There was no sign of an accompanying skeleton. It had probably been carried here by a dog. Reg did a 'Poor Yorick' bit. In Luanda's hot and humid climate and with the attentions of animal predators, bodies were quickly reduced to bones.

■ Corpses became so commonplace in the *muçeques* and suburbs after a few weeks of the continuous battle between the MPLA and FNLA that passersby usually ignored them.

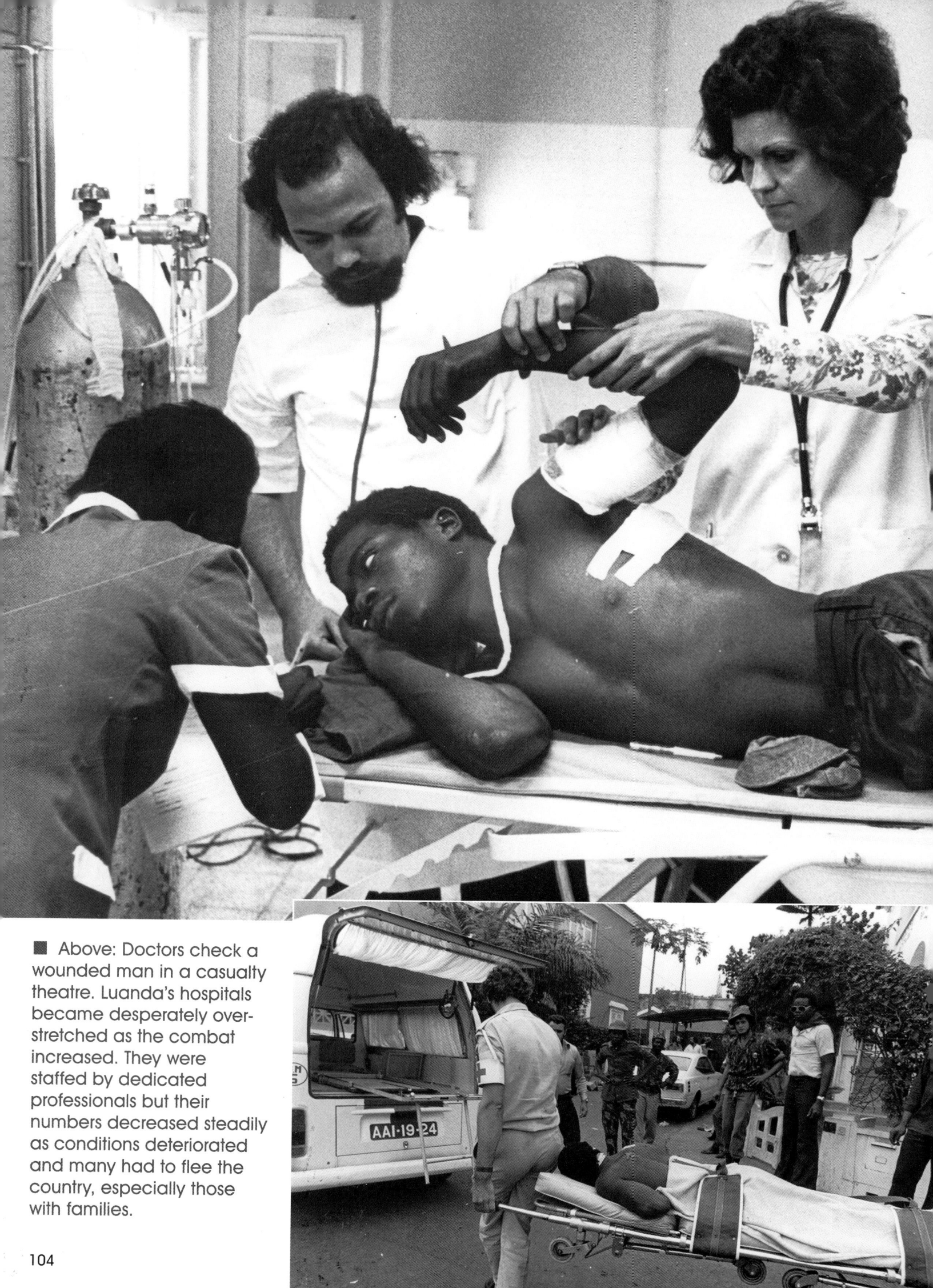

■ Above: Doctors check a wounded man in a casualty theatre. Luanda's hospitals became desperately over-stretched as the combat increased. They were staffed by dedicated professionals but their numbers decreased steadily as conditions deteriorated and many had to flee the country, especially those with families.

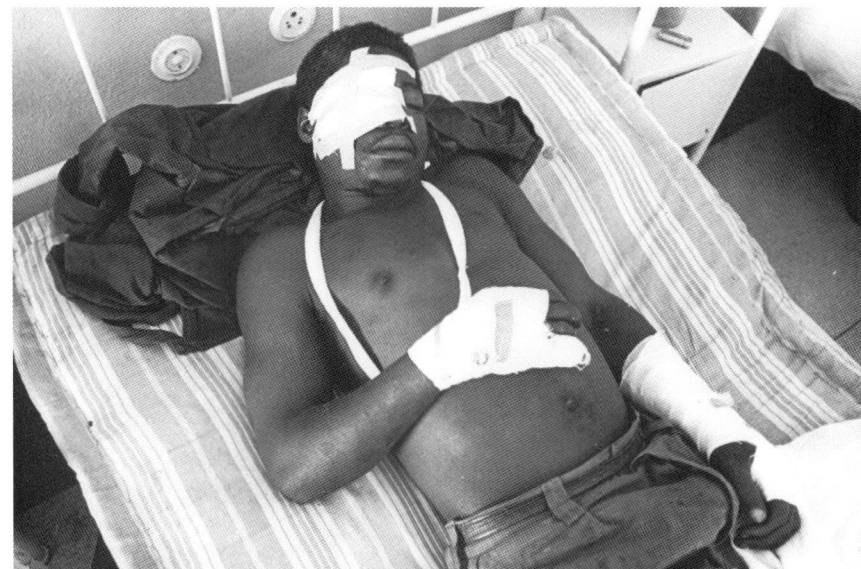

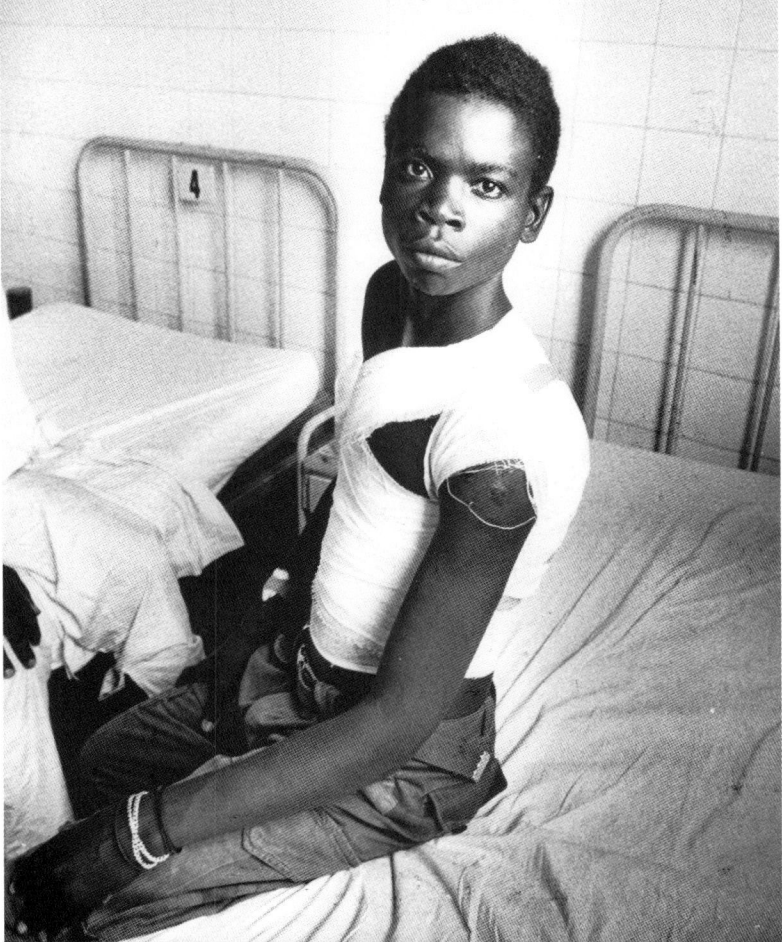

■ Left and below: Lucky to be alive, each has sustained three serious wounds. In both cases the men are thankfully asleep, probably dopey with morphine.

■ Left: For the time being, this young guerrilla's war is over.

■ Left: People shot in the fighting were lucky if they got medical help, like this man wounded in a suburb who was taken to hospital by ambulance, an ever rarer sight in the city.

WATERSHED

By mid-1975 we had stopped using the Tivoli Hotel and moved into the luxurious Tropico a few minutes away. Some peculiar people, whites, had begun moving into the Tivoli. They were Soviet advisers to the MPLA. This was not a good place for Western journalists.

Using our small office nearby became an ordeal when refugees, swarming into the city centre from the *muçeques*, discovered the building. The mezzanine floor filled with several score people – men, women and children. They were miserable, clad in rags and were hungry. Some of the women were breast-feeding babies.

They moved lethargically to make space when we appeared at the top of the stairs, murmuring greetings. It was tangible tragedy right under our noses but there was nothing we could do for them. Most of the offices were closed. The refugees made no attempt to break into them to steal anything. They sat and did nothing

More and more moved into our building. The situation became untenable. They had discovered the toilets on the mezzanine but did not know how to flush the pans. Within days the overflow of sewage began leaking out the door and trickling down the stairs.

There was little to do in the evenings. No one in his right mind went walkabout outside the immediate city centre.

Crowds thronged the sidewalk cafés along the Marginal. They ate huge crayfish, prawns and other seafood delicacies and washed them down with fine wines but the atmosphere was fraught with anxiety. The waiters were nervous. They tried to chase away dozens of young street children in the shadows at the edge of the mosaic-paved sidewalk.

These were refugees from the *muçeques*, bony, thinly clothed and too frightened to beg. They watched every forkful with hungry eyes.

Sometimes a diner would hold out a crayfish tail or some other snack. The kids scampered close to snatch like jackals at a kill.

■ Refugees from the fighting on Luanda's streets.

■ Above left: Luanda was in a mess. Public servics like street cleaning had vanished. The water supply was intermittent – interrupted frequently when workers at the Quifandongo pump station fled from the battle there between the MPLA and the FNLA. These people are collecting water from one of the lowest taps in town, on Waterfront street, because the supply was so weak it could not reach their household taps higher up.

■ Above: As in Lourenço Marques, Luandans queued to draw their now severely devalued money from banks.

■ Left: A young woman walks to her job past the growing mound of rubbish on the sidewalks.

At this stage, a few months before independence day, the MPLA was virtually in full control of Luanda although clashes still occurred between them and pockets of FNLA in some of the *muçeques*. Hot fighting continued between the two on the outskirts of the city and at a number of other places in northern Angola, all too remote and hazardous to visit. Even the Red Cross travelled with extreme caution.

So confident was the MPLA now that they ramped up their recruitment and training in the townships, where they were struggling to impose a measure of law and order.

The training was rudimentary at best and without proper weapons, but there was no shortage of enthusiastic recruits. Many children wanted to join in the fun with mock guns made of wood and scraps, some wearing camouflage uniforms cut down from Portuguese issue.

The MPLA guerrillas were their only role models in a chaotic world. To its credit, the MPLA let them play and there is no evidence that they ever used child soldiers.

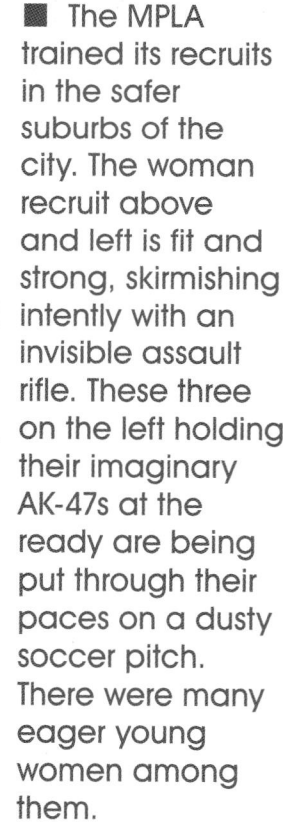

■ The MPLA trained its recruits in the safer suburbs of the city. The woman recruit above and left is fit and strong, skirmishing intently with an invisible assault rifle. These three on the left holding their imaginary AK-47s at the ready are being put through their paces on a dusty soccer pitch. There were many eager young women among them.

■ The MPLA instructors did not pussyfoot with their recruits. Walking across their taut stomachs was a way to weed out the weak and strengthen the strong.

WATERSHED

■ "Down, *camarada*, down! They're shooting at you!" A raw recruit gets right down to it at an MPLA boot camp in Luanda, using an old bolt-action rifle, probably a Mauser. Most recruits were unsophisticated folk with no experience of soldiering and had to be taught from the very basics up, including what gunsights were for and how to use them.

■ Above: The standard way to teach men to leopard crawl, straight out of the army textbook, though they did not fire live ammunition over them.

■ Left: A recruit doing the assault course on the training ground.

■ Every bit the young soldiers, two boys march smartly on the parade ground with their wooden AK-47s.

■ Above: The MPLA did not appear to recruit children as happened later in Sierra Leone and Uganda. But they sensibly harnessed their enthusiasm to make them work at being young cadets, starting with parade-ground drill. No schools were functioning and it helped to keep them out of mischief – and perhaps prepare them for recruitment when they were old enough.

■ Left: Cadets on parade. Their AK-47s are wooden and the piece of drainpipe is in lieu of an RPG launcher.

■ Above: This boy's home-made gun can actually shoot using a nail as a firing pin and a piece of elastic to drive it. It is as much danger to the shooter as to his target.

■ Left: Wearing an almost perfect copy of a Portuguese camouflage uniform, a cadet gives a smart salute to a military policeman.

October 1975 was a depressing month. I watched the death of a country I had grown very fond of, a place of great beauty and potential. It rotted and fell apart.

It had deteriorated drastically in the past two or three months. Far from inspiring celebration, the imminence of independence was generating only anger, fear and chaos. The gloom was pervasive.

The FNLA was positioning its much larger forces for a major attack from the north and east. Its aim was to force the MPLA into a negotiated settlement before independence, thus hoping to gain a large share in government and a presence in Luanda. UNITA was not even in the picture.

Many people believed Luanda was about to become a battleground. Most diplomats had prudently departed, leaving caretaker personnel. The South African consulate-general had shut down completely. Regardless of who gained power, they would not be welcome.

Angola was seeing the biggest human evacuation by air, sea and road in African history, the sad and ignoble final departure of Portugal from Africa. Portuguese civilians were fleeing en masse. Abandoning their homes, people streamed into Luanda from outlying villages and farms in trucks, cars, tractors and trailers heaped with luggage – caravans of fear. They ran the gauntlet of trigger-happy rebels for hundreds of kilometres. Many people farther away from Luanda headed for their nearest border.

■ For many people, the only places to shelter were the pavements and gutters. None could afford hotel prices even if accommodation was available. Some came to Luanda because as MPLA supporters they had found themselves beging targeted by the FNLA or UNITA.

■ Luanda streets became 'home' to hundreds of people, black and white, who fled outlying villages and farms in the hope of finding transport out of the country, like this family who settled on a sidewalk.

■ Now in control of the city, the MPLA and its supporters continued to parade their flags through the streets.

■ Refugees from Nova Lisboa (left), the central Angolan city ravaged by almost continuous fighting between the guerrilla movements, gather at the airport for transport to Luanda to board flights to other countries. Fleeing Nova Lisboans say their farewells to those who dare to stay as luggage is loaded on their flight (right).

The mass airlift was a surprisingly efficient operation. It would be completed by the end of October and in the first few days of November the planes would depart with their support personnel, "rolling up the carpet behind them and switching off the lights," said one observer.

American, Russian, East and West German, British and French aircraft had already helped Portugal's TAP airline and its air force to move out 140,000 Portuguese and had about 30,000 left.

About 90,000 more went on scheduled flights to Portugal and South Africa, about 20,000 crossed into South West Africa overland and many thousands more flew or sailed to places like Brazil or simply crossed into neighbouring Zaire or Zambia.

Only about 30,000 whites out of nearly half a million would stay in Angola, according to Portuguese officials.

Hundreds of lorries and cars queued on the road to the dockyard packed with crates labelled 'Portugal'.

On 10 November the last of the 9,000 or so Portuguese troops still in Angola would board ship or plane for home, leaving behind a sizeable stock of military vehicles, a few small naval patrol boats, several old transport planes and some weapons. Meanwhile, they were under orders to fight only if attacked.

Portugal was abandoning Angola. The country was destined to be another East–West proxy battleground. Already there was evidence of direct involvement in the troubles here by outside powers.

The scene at Luanda's airport was grimly depressing: a motley, grubby crowd of thousands waited in steamy heat to be crammed aboard aircraft – husbands and wives, flocks of weary children clutching treasured toys. The terminal area was littered with ornaments and other baggage air crews had made them abandon because of space and weight restrictions. They were also body-searched and made to surrender knives and guns.

■ Youngsters flown to Luanda in a light aircraft make their way to the terminal to wait for the next flight out.

The children's faces say it all: where to now? Some of them guard luggage that there is no way they'll be able to take with them. Flights were crowded and weight restrictions limited them to the minimum of personal possessions.

■ Left: Royal Air Force personnel checked the luggage of every one of the thousands they took out of Angola, relieving them of knives like this one and guns and other weapons.

■ Below: Grief at leaving half a lifetime behind with a future unknown.

WATERSHED

One man's misery is another man's profit. Some entrepeneurs made hay out of the mass exodus by buying valuables from departing Portuguese for a few US dollars.

The driver of a big, almost new Mercedes Benz parked at the roadside at the airport among abandoned vehicles and locked the doors. A wheeler-dealer offered him $50 for the car keys. The man shrugged and handed them over. The buyer drove the car to a chartered freighter in the harbour.

Shortly before independence day the high commissioner, Admiral Cardoso, told journalists that the military had removed all their equipment except a small helicopter which had mysteriously gone missing. It had been sold.

Central Luanda became slightly safer in October. The MPLA were struggling with the unfamiliar business of running a city. Travelling outside was hazardous. Scheduled flights to other centres had long since ceased

The unmistakeable thudding of distant artillery was audible from the top floor dining room of the Tropico Hotel. From there we could see smoke far to the north in the direction of the Quifandongo water pump station.

Reg Shay and I followed the road north in the hope of getting closer to the action. We were slowed to walking pace amid a growing crowd of soldiers, all armed and striding the same way, all summoned to battle. We were stopped by a tall MPLA guerrilla in camouflage fatigues and beret. He hefted a large machine gun and was festooned with belts of ammunition.

We could not go on, he said. He was polite and apologetic, but adamant. We turned back.

Had we been able to continue we would have reached not a frontline but a defence barrier of MPLA forces confronting unseen FNLA artillery several kilometres to the north. This was just one of many long-range skirmishes between them for control of Quifandongo.

The rising confrontation brought a last-ditch attempt by Lisbon to find compromise. They sent out Admiral Victor Crespo, who had presided at the handover of Mozambique and now had the singularly wishful title of Minister for Inter-territorial Cooperation.

He criss-crossed Angola to meet the three rebel leaders but no one had the slightest hope he would succeed. The civil war had begun and nothing could stop it. To underline this the FNLA announced in Carmona, where it had its military headquarters, that it was setting up its own government for Angola to counter the MPLA and had appointed some ministers.

It was at this time – 22 October – that the name South Africa first came into the picture.

It was raised by the MPLA's shadow finance minister, Saidy Minga, after the MPLA issued a communiqué in which they admitted, for the first time, that they were having difficulty holding the southern Angolan territory they had seized from UNITA.

The reason, Minga said, was "a massive invasion of the territory by South African forces" which had already captured the small town of Chibia only 30 kilometres from the southern capital, Sa da Bandeira.

"We have fought South African troops and we will continue to do so," he said. "We are fighting South Africa, Zaire, the FNLA and UNITA together. Two and a half million people in South Africa cannot make wars everywhere in Africa. They think they can kill and destroy everywhere in Africa but we will fight them."

I doubt any of the foreign correspondents or diplomatic observers believed his rhetoric, although all reported it. It looked like an MPLA attempt to make excuses for setbacks. It would be ridiculous for South Africa to involve itself in this disastrous mess ... or so we believed.

In fact Minga was right. South Africa had invaded, both in the south and, although he did not say so, in the north.

Washington had given its covert agreement for South Africa to enter the fray against the threat by the dreaded communist-backed MPLA – greatly overblown by the South African government.

P. W. Botha was suddenly in military heaven. He unleashed a strike force of several hundred infantry backed by Panhard armoured cars which penetrated deep into southern Angola at astonishing speed. It aimed directly at the MPLA to support UNITA.

In Luanda we knew none of this. It was done behind a screen of total censorship and flat denial in South Africa and was launched from north of the Red Line in South West Africa – an area barred to observers where the military could operate with impunity.

What my team did pick up, however, was word that a strange group of foreigners had landed on the coast about 40 kilometres south of Luanda, near the mouth of the Cuanza River. Allen Pizzey heard rumours they were Cubans, which we also found hard to believe.

"Go and look," I told Allen and photographer Peter Jordan. They set off in the morning and came back late that afternoon dishevelled and weary. It had been a hairy trip past roadblocks manned by MPLA guerrillas full of truculence and suspicion. Allen sweet-talked his way through and they found a large man, apparently an officer, in unfamiliar camouflage kit smoking a huge cigar while he supervised the ferrying of equipment across the river, where a blown bridge had been repaired.

He could have passed for Portuguese but Allen had no doubt he was Cuban. He amiably shrugged off questions in English and Portuguese, apparently unable to understand either and gave his orders in what sounded to Allen like Spanish. Peter got a picture and they rode the gauntlet back to Luanda.

This was the first visible confirmation that Cuba was sending troops to help the MPLA. They numbered about 700, we later established, and had brought weaponry to train the MPLA.

It was also the last of our treks outside the city. Travel was too risky. Conditions in Luanda suddenly worsened. Taps gurgled and ran dry. The supply stopped because technicians at the pump station had fled.

There were few cats in Luanda, if any. They were too edible. In the ghost city of Nova Lisboa dog was on the menu. Hunger was commonplace as the old Angola went out not with a bang but with a scream of anguish.

When the wind was right we could hear the war from the hotel, the solid thump of mortar or artillery shells being delivered about 30 kilometres to the north.

Outside hotels life was a jungle. Luanda, once Portugal's largest city after Lisbon and Oporto, was dying. The once lovely capital was already littered with tombstones of wrecked and abandoned cars in nearly every street, dead-eyed houses and paint-daubed monuments. In the evenings a few traffic policemen still, miraculously, appeared on point duty and, equally miraculously, were obeyed.

In the last days of October the fighting grew so hot that Luandans feared FNLA forces might break into the city at any moment, which would have unleashed killing on a genocidal scale when they encountered the teeming pro-MPLA hordes in the *muçeques*.

On 24 October the MPLA issued a call-up throughout Angola to all men between 18 and 35 to combat what it termed "a foreign invasion in the pay of international imperialism".

Next day, 25 October, the FNLA halted its armoured drive toward the city from the north and began moving forces to the east and south in an effort to cut Luanda off completely from the rest of Angola.

Things began to happen fast. *The Times* of London reported from Lusaka that Cuban troops were being shipped into Angola – confirming what Allen and Peter had already discovered.

In Luanda Commander Juju, chief of staff of the MPLA's army, FAPLA, announced at a press conference that South African forces had invaded the southern Huila and Cunene provinces and partly occupied the southern city of Sa da Bandeira, a major crossroads and commercial and agricultural centre.

■ A Cuban soldier directs a truck carrying arms across the Cuanza River, about 40 kilometres south of Luanda, the first proof that Cubans had entered the fray.

The pistol-packing Juju said the South Africans, together with forces from Zaire, were under the banner of the UNITA and FNLA movements.

This was carried by our newspapers in South Africa without comment from the authorities there.

Suddenly the balance was shifting. UNITA and the FNLA were launching attacks on MPLA strongholds and outposts in several widespread areas north, south and east of the capital. Sa da Bandeira had fallen completely to the attackers.

Andy Jaffe of *Newsweek* magazine was the first to get confirmation that the invasion was by South African forces. He spoke to Portuguese soldiers evacuated to Luanda from the south. They said the men who seized Sa da Bandeira were South African regular troops, men in armoured cars backed by infantry who, within days, captured the ports of Moçamedes, Lobito and Benguela and some inland centres.

We briskly reported South Africa's astonishing and spectacular intervention but not a word of it appeared in our newspapers, unknown to those of us in Luanda because no one had told us about the censorship. They used our reports but carefully omitted direct mention of South African involvement.

We wrote that in Luanda "MPLA sources still insist that the captors of Moçamedes and Sa da Bandeira included regular South African forces with helicopters but this is discounted by the Portuguese authorities".

By 30 October the FNLA and UNITA had launched a widespread, coordinated attack to try to crack the MPLA's grip on more than half of Angola. Their combined force of at least 50,000 were ranged against an estimated 30,000 MPLA troops on at least seven fronts spread right through the country.

"The Angola situation is clearly moving towards a major, all-out showdown," we reported, although in a country larger than South Africa battles would be localized.

There was no longer any doubt that outsiders were involved.

"The company of Portuguese troops stationed at Moçamedes to supervise and protect the evacuation of refugees from there has met and identified them."

Most were Portuguese but English-speakers were among them. They were well disciplined, they took Moçamedes without a fight and there was no looting.

"Uniformed whites have also been seen at Carmona in the north, FNLA headquarters."

By now our editors had confirmed from their own sources that South African troops had indeed invaded Angola. It was impossible to conceal – the word of mouth spread rapidly from national servicemen to their families

The editors were able to partially slip around the barriers of censorship by quoting other 'authoritative' sources as alleging South Africans were there, but could not state that as fact. The government finally admitted it to them privately but threatened dire consequences for any newspaper thst reported the truth.

What was happening was that South African troops were spearheading a predominantly UNITA counter-attack with an FNLA component that rolled back the MPLA like an old carpet. The MPLA's problem, Allen Pizzey and I reported, was that it tried to grab too much. "Its forces are spread very thin and in some areas are easily beaten when its opponents, after months of gathering strength, retaliate."

Two days before independence I reported: "Angola will die formally on Tuesday. Another thousand will die in the bloody carnage of a civil war unprecedented in Black Africa.

"An estimated 10,000 people, mostly civilians, have been killed in the past year. The figure is probably double that, with 10,000 in Luanda alone, and this is only a foretaste of what is to come.

"Tuesday, 11 November is Independence Day when at 0001 in the morning Angola finally becomes free after five centuries of Portuguese colonial rule.

"The last Portuguese authorities will not be there, having prudently sailed away in a frigate on the evening of 10 November after lowering their flag for the last time at the ancient white-walled fortress of St Miguel overlooking Luanda, the capital.

"A winner-takes-all is unavoidable now. Even if the contestants want to treat for peace – which they do not – it is too late because now Big Powers are involved. Angola has become a mini-Vietnam, an East–West battlefield."

■ Above: Portuguese troops went out of their way to help rural people even before the Lisbon coup ended their war there, helping the crippled, giving lifts to the elderly and making friends with the locals.

■ Right: Savimbi and UNITA's secretary-general, Nzau Puna.

WATERSHED

At this stage the FNLA was only 32 kilometres north of Luanda at the Bengo River, in a position to shell the city's pump station at Quifandongo, and the South African-spearheaded UNITA forces were swiftly moving north.

How fast they were moving we did not know. Later I learned that an advance South African reconnaisance force had come to almost within sight of Luanda.

Had they tried to invade the city they would have had to carve through the city's surrounding dense warrens of *muçeques* packed with fanatic and armed supporters of the MPLA. The killing would have been wholesale.

I never found out why the South Africans stopped there – perhaps because an embarrassed America withdrew its support, perhaps because supply lines were overstretched.

What we in Luanda did not know then was that South Africans were also spearheading the FNLA thrust from the north.

Weeks earlier, after the FNLA had gained control of most of the territory north of Luanda, a special South African team was landed secretly on the coast near Ambriz or Ambrizete from a submarine escorted there by a frigate. Their job was to assist the FNLA. More had probably entered Angola from Zaire, whose President Mobutu had a close, though covert, relationship with the South Africans.

One of those landed was Brigadier Ben Roos, who knew Angola like the back of his hand. He was one of the straightest, most honest men I have met.

He was an artilleryman so they sent him to the FNLA to teach them how to use their heavy weaponry. It was, he told me later, an uphill battle. The FNLA had a frustrating mishmash of big guns of varying calibres from many sources so that finding matching ammunition became a major headache. Teaching the FNLA's troops how to use them was an even bigger headache, the officers were arrogant, conceited and thought they knew it all.

Somehow Ben managed to coax, cajole and whip an artillery team into reasonable shape with the personal blessing of Mobutu. They were assigned to attack Luanda through Quifandongo.

While I was trying to cover the fighting from the south, Ben and his men were lobbing shells our way from the north. When I told him this much later he bought me a beer.

However, Ben and his FNLA team were routed by the MPLA. After weeks of stalemate, the MPLA had brought up a couple of batteries of Stalin Organs – multiple 122mm rocket launchers mounted on the platforms of trucks. These very simple but highly effective weapons developed during the Second World War could not be aimed as accurately as conventional guns but could be fired rapidly in salvoes of dozens. They carried powerful warheads to blanket large areas in devastation.

As Ben described it, his team were firing away at the MPLA lines with their various guns when suddenly the air above them seemed to split open with nerve-shattering thunder. It was the roar of Russian rockets rushing overhead. Luckily they exploded behind the artillery lines.

But the damage was done. The FNLA men had never experienced anything like this before. The noise terrified them. As more and more rockets screamed above, the FNLA abandoned their guns and fled. Ben and a handful were left behind. There was no point in continuing.

He and some other South Africans were later evacuated from the coast to a submarine in a hairy night operation, another untold story of the Angolan war.

At this point, a couple of days before independence, I too had to leave Luanda in a hurry aboard the last RAF refugee flight to Lisbon. I had been marked outside the Tropico Hotel by a group of MPLA youth. "That's the South African," one said in Portuguese, pointing at me.

The message was obvious: get the hell out of here. This was no place for South Africans while their countrymen were attacking. I left that afternoon.

In January 1976 I hitched a lift from Lusaka, Zambia, on a Lear jet lent to Jonas Savimbi by British entrepeneur Tiny Rowlands to the small town of Silva Porto in east–central Angola where Savimbi was to hold a rally.

He and his secretary-general, Nzau Puna, told an open-air gathering of a couple of hundred local Africans not to be concerned by the disappearance of the South African

forces from there. The war was turning from conventional to guerrilla, he said, and UNITA was going back to bush tactics, its real field of expertise.

Savimbi and Puna were very similar, burly men with bushy black beards wearing jungle camouflage and berets. They had been delivering the same message at villages up and down the so-called frontline between UNITA and MPLA forces coming from the north.

Four or five of us journalists were taken to see soldiers UNITA had captured. In the back room of a lonely brick building we found four small, frightened men huddled against a wall, all Cubans.

None of us could speak Spanish. I tried the only Spanish I remembered from my brief visit there – *"Buenos dias señors"* – their faces lit up pathetically with hope. We managed to get across the message with a mix of gestures, words and sketches that we were foreign journalists and would report about them. I asked them to write their names and home addresses in my notebook, which they did.

And then we had to leave. I have no idea what became of them. I gave their names and story to the Red Cross. I don't know whether they survived or fell victim to the casual African contempt for lives. Months later a number of Cubans fell into South African hands and were brought to Pretoria.

During that night we correspondents were taken by bus to the airport at Nova Lisboa, now called Huambo. Whatever Savimbi wanted us to see there we will never know. In the early dawn the town below the terminal sparkled with gunfire: the MPLA was attacking.

A former Angolan Airways Fokker Friendship landed and we scrambled aboard and got away before the fighting reached the terminal.

That was my last visit to Angola.

■ He has a pellet gun, he has cartridges although they are for a shotgun. He has pride. That was all the MPLA gave this young man: no future.

PART IV
MUÇEQUES

The most distinctive feature of the developing world is the growth around cities of huge human concentrations – sometimes suddenly, like mushrooms, sometimes over years like forests. They have various names according to country, the politest being townships, settlements or slums.

They are the problem-rich result of the mass migrations from the rural to urban areas in the past 50 to 60 years. They are caused by the rapid evolution of economies and technology during that time which made city life compelling to burgeoning populations for whom subsistence agriculture was no longer viable.

They represent the gulf between the haves and the have-nots. Not so much between rich and poor as between ignorant and educated, the trained and untrained, the sophisticates and the plebeian.

These are crucibles where the heat and pressure of survival force people to use any means, from crime to capitalism, to scramble free. They exist in many Third World countries but most visibly in Africa where the urban drift became a torrent and the slums are the largest, like the twenty or so engulfing Nairobi, said to be collectively the biggest in Africa.

Many are foyers of hell, among the most dangerous places on earth. Some have evolved into stable communities with distinctive personalities like Johannesburg's Soweto and Alexandra.

The townships of Portuguese Africa had their own characteristics. They hardly existed in Portuguese Guinea, a tiny swamp colony with little urban area to speak of, but grew abundantly around the capitals of Angola and Mozambique, Luanda and Lourenço Marques, now Maputo. In neither was there any real planning and they spread as haphazardly as any village in the African bush. In LM they were a mix of tin shanties, grass huts and low-cost brick houses of the poorer quarters.

In Luanda the modern central city spread out into middle- and lower-income suburbs. As it spread, the vacant spaces between the suburbs widened. In April 1974, at the time of the Lisbon coup, they were not vacant but jammed with slums, an ugly blend of brick, lath-and-plaster, tin and reed houses and huts with some buildings of two or more storeys scattered among them. They were models of insanitary

■ Patrolling the *muçeques* was a trip through a desolation of bombed and burned buildings; these are in one of the better-class fringes whose occupants were the first targets of the newly liberated masses.

■ An aerial view of part of a Luanda slum. An unplanned, crowded mass of buildings linked by a few roads and innumerable alleys, mostly too narrow for vehicles. Most buildings were of cement brick or mud with tin roofs. Communal taps were scarce, in some parts as few as one per thousand people.

disorganization, sweating with African humanity drawn to the bright city lights like flies to dung.

They were known as *muçeques*. Their population was estimated at half a million.

The division between the main city and its dozen or so *muçeques* was sharp and clear: this was civilization, wealth and luxury, the white-collar world; that was poverty, dirt, the source of cheap labour, the blue-collar and shirtless world. Race was less a division than class and culture but black prejudice against whites as the colonizers was strong.

The old regime simply ignored the *muçeques*. If they gave trouble the notorious political police, the DGS, soon heard and crushed it ruthlessly. With it they crushed human hope.

Then came the Lisbon coup. With the political police gone the lid of repression was blown off by an excess of reaction. A huge rise in expectations poisoned by fanatic political competition drove the unsophisticated masses into fury.

Law and order ceased to exist. Life became a hellish saga of survival against enemies and hunger. The *muçeques* became the urban heart of the warfare that tore the city and eventually the country apart.

The trading stores and homes of the whites and mulattos who lived there were looted or burned. Many of the communal taps dried up. Streets were blocked by rubble and wrecked cars. Nights were punctuated by gunfire.

■ Above: Portuguese soldiers stand guard on the roof of a trader's home and shop while he loads his few remaining possessions to flee to safety from the rampaging mobs.

■ Above right: A *muçeque* resident enjoys his prize, a chair looted from a trader's home.

■ Left: The troops had to guard firefighters who came to douse the blazes that sprang up all over the *muçeques*, a task made exceedingly difficult by the tight, twisting alleys and the lack of water sources. Eventually the firemen and troops gave up.

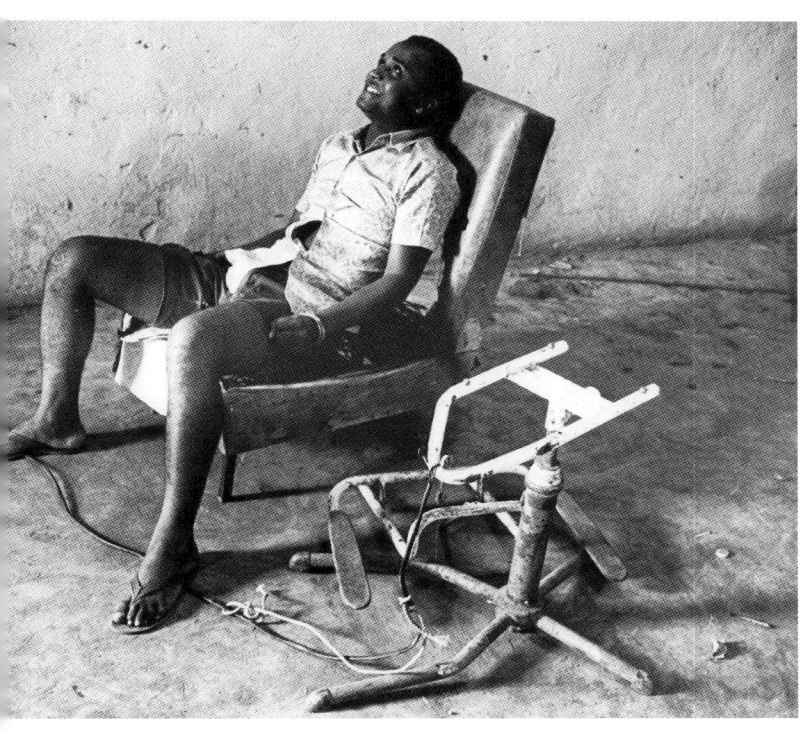

A young officer commanding a Portuguese patrol about to go into the *muçeques* said I could ride with them. The soldiers made space for me on their troop carrier, two park benches mounted back-to-back on the flatbed of a Unimog truck. They all wore camouflage and carried G3 rifles, loaded and cocked. I carried my Leica, loaded and cocked.

The patrol was an eye-opener.

Three Africans fled when we rounded the corner and bore down on them. They ran through the shattered doors of an abandoned house so pocked by bullets the scene looked like Berlin 1945, and then vanished down an alley.

"They run when they see us because they have guilty consciences," said the sergeant beside me, his automatic rifle poised.

The blacks in the teeming, poverty-ridden *muçeques* did not show any conscience. The widespread death and destruction had given them arrogance. With the collapse of colonialism they had power and they knew it.

Their first expression of it was against whites. Whites who ventured unescorted into the narrow, dusty alleys would die. Killing a white man made a black man a hero.

In a road fringing the Rangel *muçeque*, scene of the worst violence, Africans stared sullenly or simply ignored us. A few taunted and laughed at the soldiers, who grinned back amiably.

The Unimog with a pair of park benches on the platform, here travelling one of the 'streets', was the army's main form of troop carrier.

WATERSHED

■ Left: *Muçeque* dwellers such as these in a tin-shanty street became so used to passing Portuguese patrols they ignored them.

■ Below: Children, who often started trouble by stoning cars, hoisted fists in the black power salute favoured by the MPLA, like the boy on the right. Here they cheer and taunt a passing army patrol, one wielding a toy pistol cowboy style, another holding a wooden gun.

"Unless there is trouble we will not drive into the heart of the *muçeque*, down those alleys," said Second Lieutenant Vitor Martins.

The alleys twisted between packed rows of mud, brick or ramshackle tin homes. Pools of filthy water, garbage and worse edged them, for there was no proper sanitation.

Several were blocked by barricades of tree trunks, rubble from buildings and burned cars.

How people survived in such wretched conditions, God knew. A reason for the violence was they had nothing to lose.

Lieutenant Martins pointed to a big wild fig tree about 100 metres away. "Someone got up there and shot at our soldiers with a Kalashnikov," he said. "He killed one of them. We shot him out of the tree."

We came to another troop carrier as a screaming black man was being hauled on board. An angry gesticulating crowd of African men and women looked on.

The yelling swelled when one exasperated soldier punched the prisoner, for what I could not tell.

"The Africans will have seen which company those troops belong to," said Martins, "and they will attack it whenever they can."

■ The filthy, crowded side alleys weaving through the *muçeques* were death traps for the unwary where only the residents knew the borders between ethnic groups and rebel movements. The hulks of cars, the fate of whose owners was unknown, made them inaccessible except to the locals and troops in armoured vehicles.

■ The locals went about their daily business as if nothing had happened, so accustomed had they become after a few weeks to wholesale destruction. By night they battened themselves indoors unless out on the hunt.

■ The destruction was awesome. Scores of buildings were gutted by fire and some literally torn to pieces. Not one of the white-owned trading stores was untouched.

Later I walked down the short Avenida do Brasil in central Luanda. It took only ten minutes to the point where the pleasant apartment blocks and shops suddenly ceased. The avenue went on into a human hell in the infamous Rangel *muçeque*.

The MPLA took me and José Ricardo, a brilliant young Portuguese newsman, on a tour through some *muçeques* to see what they were doing to improve the lot of the inhabitants.

I had been into them several times by now but the dehumanizing abasement, the canker of poverty, the destruction and the futility of existence shocked me.

We went into 'liberated' zones. Guerrillas with loaded automatic rifles and fixed bayonets held at bay the crowds of Africans who immediately gathered around, some openly hostile.

The MPLA began a crash programme to relieve the foul conditions for the population, of whom about 90 per cent had no fixed employment and about 80 per cent were illiterate.

Their effort was pathetically inadequate. Luanda had about a dozen *muçeques* with populations from about 30,000 up.

How could they stop the rampant crime when the only way people could survive was by crime? And they needed gigantic funds and time to feed, educate and employ so many people, build decent homes and provide light, water and sanitation.

■ The alleys and backyards were the public toilets, like this one where a prancing girl grins at the camera. The inescapable impact was the stench. I could shut my eyes to the visible filth and degradation but there was no way to block out the blended odours of human excrement, rotting fish, sick-sweet garbage and the flyblown carcases of dead dogs.

■ Right: A patrol has just arrested this troublemaker who yells his defiance. The soldiers keep their guns close.

■ Above: The people at this ramshackle street market were visibly hostile when the MPLA patrol passed, probably toward the two white men with it.

■ Right: This impromptu marketplace in the grubby ruins around the sole remaining wall of what was once a trading store is dramatic. It is pockmarked by bullets or shrapnel, stained by fire and bears the inscription in crude lettering *ZONA LIBERTADA* – liberated zone. Graffiti anounces that this is the *Praça da Republica da Cazenga* – The Plaza of the Republic of Cazenga – ruled by the MPLA. They make it clear that outsiders are not welcome. The stink from the partly dried fish and chunks of unidentifiable meat was overpowering.

■ Left: She has little to smile about but this mother has managed to retain some sense of domestic order in the midst of chaos. Women were the strong survivors in the slums.

■ Facing below: The future looked bleak for these kids in the *muçeques* in 1975, when Angola was entering a civil war that lasted over 15 years. They were exuberant in the euphoria of so-called freedom, but their homes were primitive or in ruin, they had no schools, food was scarce, sickness was rife and work prospects were nil. There has been some improvement since the war ended, but very little, impeded by corruption and incompetence.

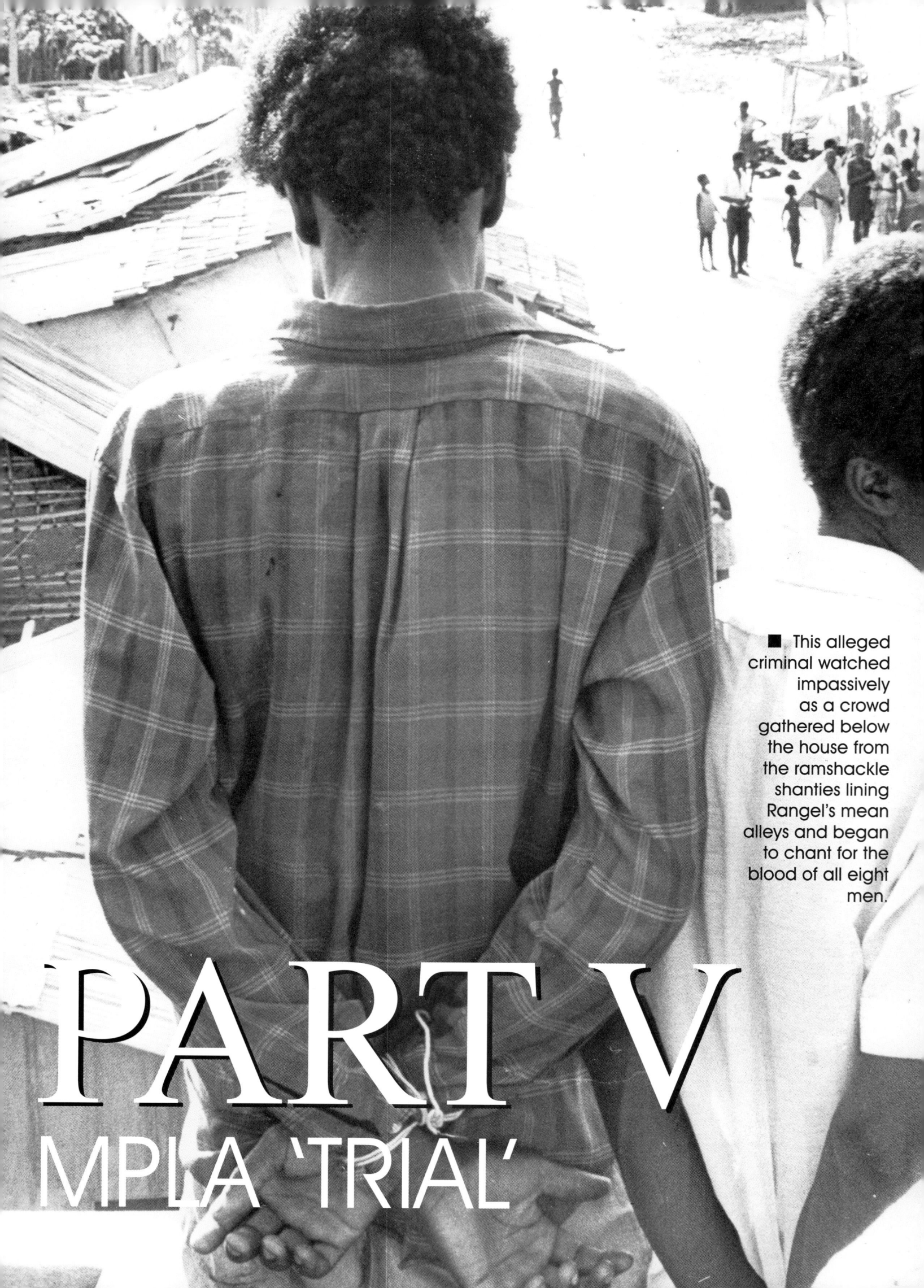

■ This alleged criminal watched impassively as a crowd gathered below the house from the ramshackle shanties lining Rangel's mean alleys and began to chant for the blood of all eight men.

PART V
MPLA 'TRIAL'

Mike Chapman, Brazilian-born Briton, long-time resident of Luanda and freelance foreign correspondent, is searched by MPLA men outside their house before the press conference. They were so thorough they took apart my ballpoint pen. At left is freelancer Reg Shay.

When they had taken control of Luanda, the MPLA began a public relations drive to show the world what they were doing to restore order to the shattered city and the lives of its shell-shocked inhabitants.

Foreign correspondents received a telephonic invitation to a press conference at 15h00 at an address in one of the city's better middle-class areas. It was the weirdest press conference I have experienced.

It began in a quiet suburb and ended in Luanda's worst no-go area, with a slavering crowd of more than a thousand people yelling for the instant death of eight men perched on a rooftop edge with their hands tied behind their backs.

I drove with about a dozen other newsmen to a small house guarded by gun-toting young men in civilian clothes. We presented our press credentials, issued by the junta government, and they carefully body-searched each of us at the garden gate before letting us in.

There was no sign of any preparation for a press conference. MPLA officials milled about gesticulating and yelling. We asked what was going on. "*Momento, momento*," they said with upraised hands, be patient.

Forty-five minutes later the things turned even stranger. A dozen or so young MPLA guerrillas in drab green, black boots and black berets, armed with assorted lethal machinery, boiled out of the house surrounding eight very nervous-looking men whom they bundled into waiting cars.

■ The agitated prisoners were shoved into a battered Land Rover and other vehicles, we were ushered into our cars and the whole party drove into the very depths of the dangerous Rangel *muçeque*.

Their hands were fastened behind their backs with cord and wire. The MPLA would now present them to the press, a spokesman said, "to show you some of the criminals we have captured who were responsible for the violence and killing and burning of the past ten days."

Countless stones lay at the sides of the broken road ready to be thrown, where barricades of tree trunks had been partly shoved aside, where entering without MPLA protection would have been suicide.

In the convoy rode the MPLA's local chiefs and, ominously, a priest. We stopped at the burned-out hulk of a three-storey brick-and-concrete building.

Men, women and hordes of hungry children ranged around us like wolves around sheep but did nothing because of the MPLA guerrillas holding them back.

We climbed narrow concrete steps up the inside wall of the building to the flat concrete rooftop. There the MPLA lined up the eight prisoners facing outward on the edge of the roof.

Erminio Escorcio, a leading MPLA figure, raised a megaphone. These were men who had done the evil things for which the MPLA was being blamed, he bellowed.

He began to intone a list of crimes they had allegedly committed. This one had killed his brother. That one had chopped up someone with a panga. Another had set a building on fire. This man had stolen from someone …

As the accusations rolled sonorously out over the battered roofs of the surrounding slum jungle, people poured from the rathole homes. They filled the open space in front of the building and crowded the streets and sidewalks.

An MPLA military chief took the megaphone and formally announced each prisoner's name and the details of his crime. Then my blood chilled.

As each name was spoken the ragtag mass of people below began to yell for his immediate execution.

I photographed the men gazing down at the crowd, their wire-bound wrists behind their backs.

Some of the captives watched the crowd impassively, even with contempt. One youngster argued bitterly until an armed guard told him to shut up. A man wept, pleading for mercy for his brother, one among the eight.

"NO!" the bloodthirsty mass bellowed when the MPLA military chief stated firmly that the eight would be handed to the Portuguese authorities for proper trial.

■ A young man, wrists bound with cord, is brought up the stairs to the open roof of the ruined house. The MPLA did not explain the injury to his nose. He is guarded by a man with a burp gun. Behind him are journalists.

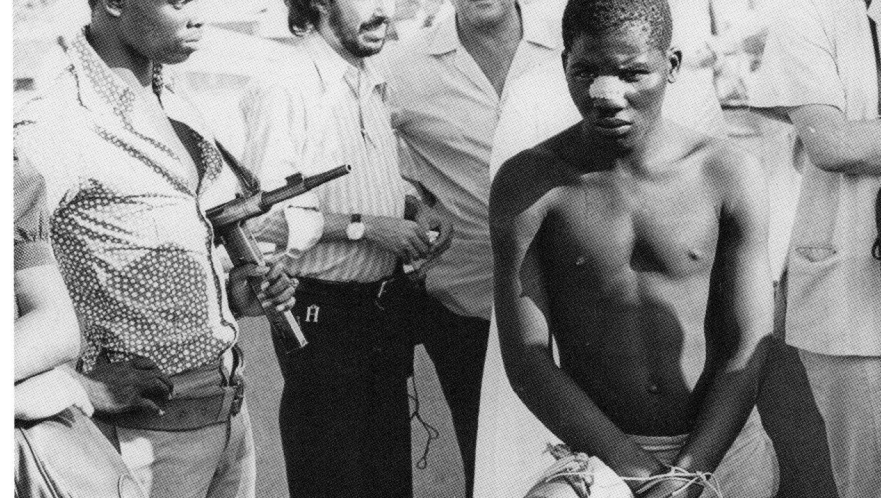

"Throw them down to us!" they roared and pressed closer to the building.

The vibes on the rooftop suddenly changed. The MPLA said gruffly we must leave right now, we would be escorted back. There was fear in the air; they were worried that the crowd would get out of hand.

We picked our way down the precarious steps and to our vehicles behind a screen of ready weapons. The prisoners came down behind us. By now the temper of the crowd had risen to a constant buzz of angry muttering. This was no place to pause. We left in something of a hurry.

On the way I pondered how eight men could be held responsible for the death and pillage that hads ravaged Luanda. I wondered, too, how many among that sickening mob were also murderers, rapists, arsonists and thieves.

The MPLA assured us their captives were handed over to the Portuguese authorities. We never received confirmation. If they were handed over they would probably have been released because in that climate of anarchy there was no functioning judicial system.

Or their captors might have taken the easy way out, quietly shot them and buried them in some backyard in the wood-and-iron jungle.

The press conference did little to improve the MPLA's image. Angels do not bind prisoners' wrists with wire or display them before a bloodthirsty mob.

> "I pondered how eight men could be held responsible for the death and pillage that had ravaged Luanda ... how many among that sickening mob were also murderers, rapists, arsonists and thieves."

■ The close-up shots show the men's wrists manacled with electrical cord and one possibly with fencing wire.

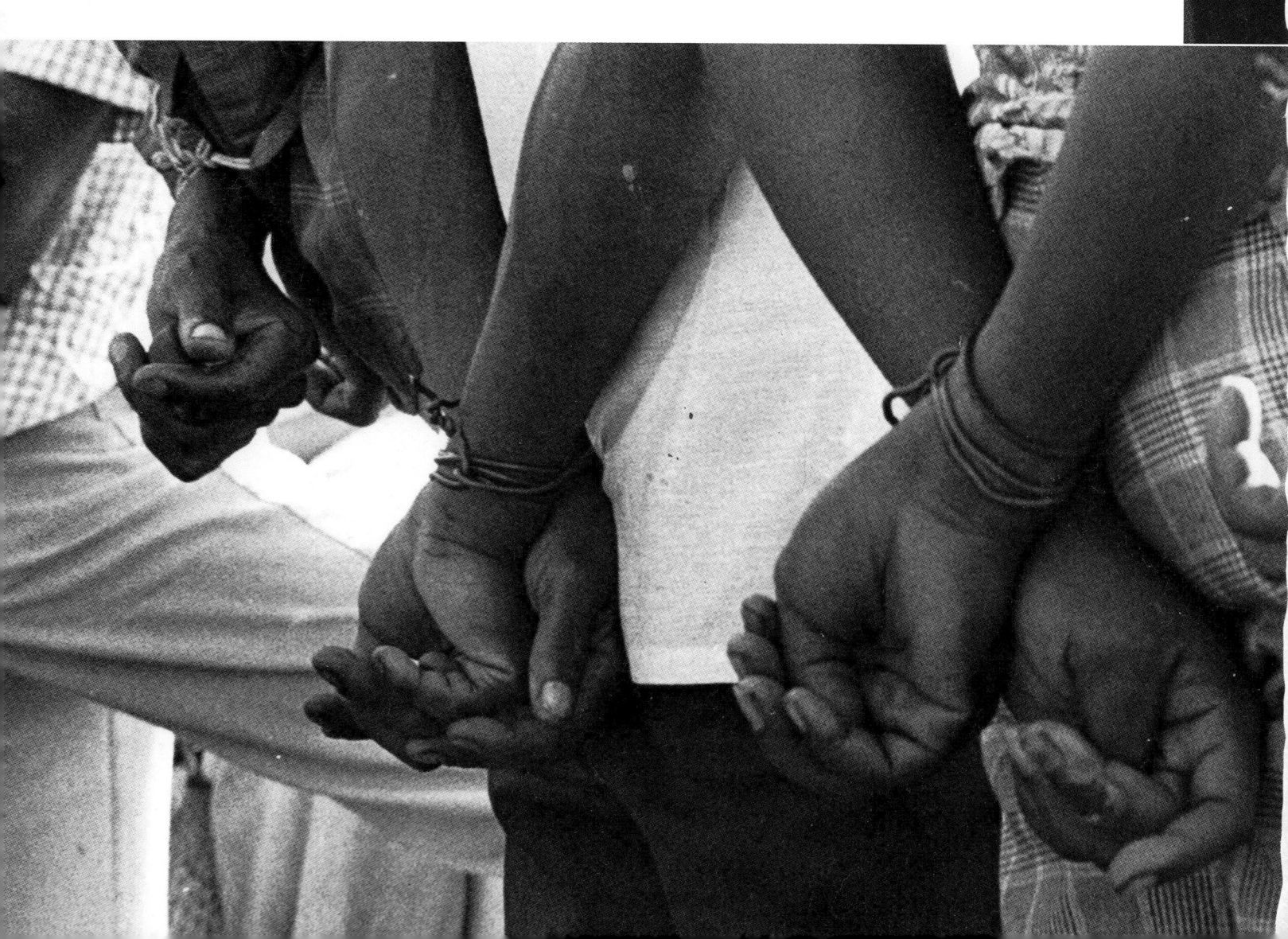

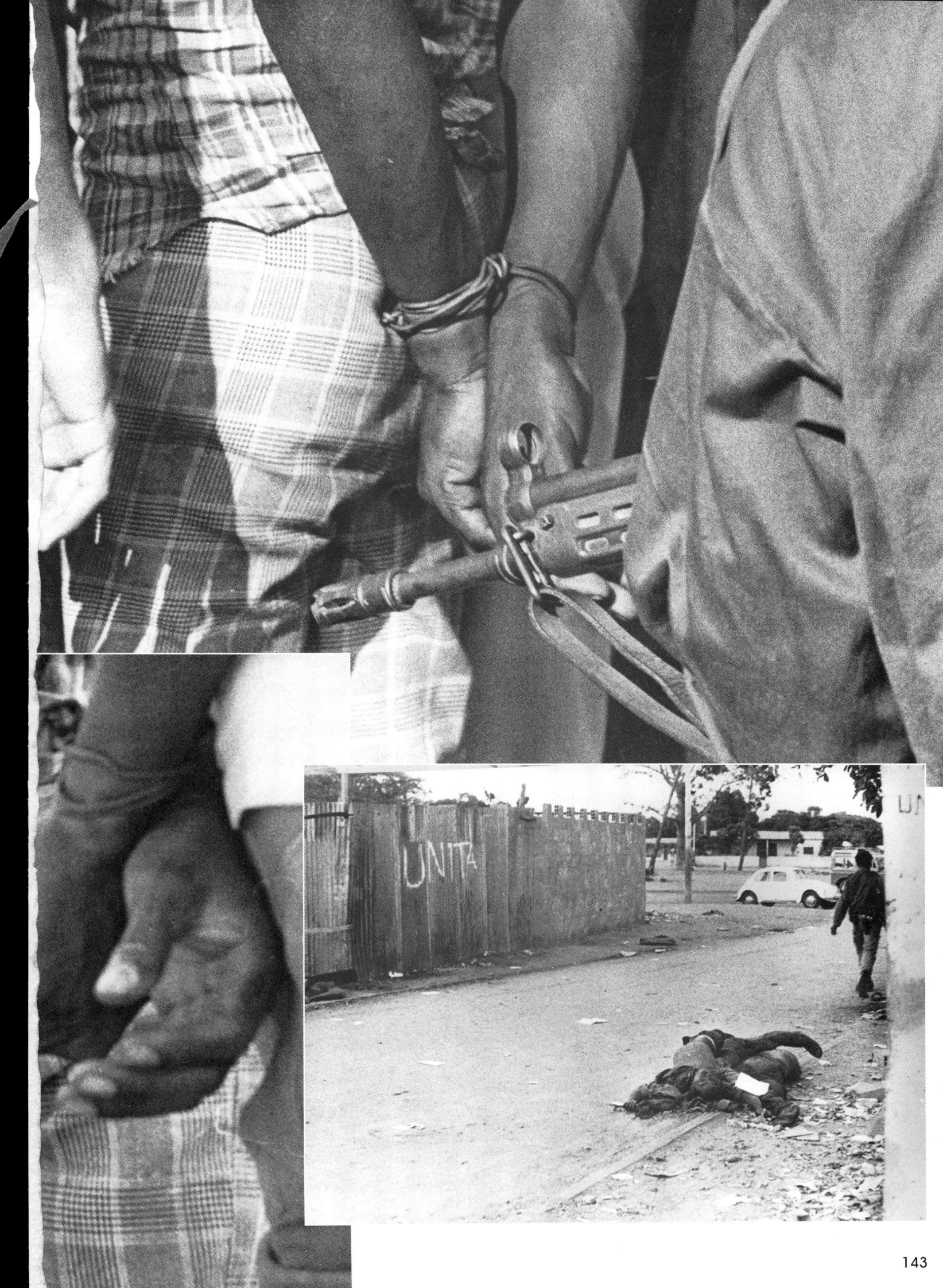